JAMES

Exploring the Elements of an Authentic Christian Lifestyle

Everett Hill

I would love to hear from you! Please send your comments about this book to info@everetth.com. Thank you.

Copyright 2016, Everett Hill. All rights reserved. Except for brief excerpts for review purposes, no part of this publication may be reproduced or used in any form without the prior written permission of the publisher.

Unless otherwise indicated, all Scripture quotations are from The Holy Bible, English Standard Version (ESV), copyright 2001 by Crossway, a publishing ministry of Good News Publishers. Used by permission. All rights reserved.

Scripture quotations marked (NLT) are taken from the Holy Bible, New Living Translation, copyright 1996, 2004, 2007 by Tyndale House Foundation. Used by permission of Tyndale House Publishers, Inc., Carol Stream, Illinois 60188. All rights reserved.

Scripture quotations marked HCSB are taken from the Holman Christian Standard Bible, Copyright 1999, 2000, 2002, 2003 by Holman Bible Publishers. Used by permission. Holman Christian Standard Bible, Holman CSB, and HCSB are federally registered trademarks of Holman Bible Publishers.

Scripture taken from The Message. Copyright 1993, 1994, 1995, 1996, 2000, 2001, 2002. Used by permission of NavPress Publishing Group.

Scripture quotations taken from the Amplified® Bible, Copyright © 2015 by The Lockman Foundation Used by permission.

Scripture quotations taken from the New American Standard Bible, Copyright 1960, 1962, 1963, 1968, 1971, 1972, 1973, 1975, 1977, 1995 by The Lockman Foundation Used by permission. (www.Lockman.org)

Dedication

To Angela:
Without you, I would be lost.

To Mia:
Thank you for helping me glimpse God the Father as I experience being your dad.

Acknowledgements

I would like to extend a huge thanks to Paula Hill, Craig Borkenhagen and John Snow for their help in editing this book. It would not be the same without them.

Table of Contents

Introduction i

James Chapter 1 1
James 1:1 – Pulling Back the Curtain 2
James 1:2-4 – Staying on Course 9
James 1:5-8 – Seeking the Wisdom of God 21
James 1:9-12 – Keeping Eternity in Our Sights 26
James 1:13-15 – Forsaking the Footsteps of Death 35
James 1:16-18 – Participating in God's Life 48
James 1:19-21 – Putting on Meekness 56
James 1:22-27 – Acting on the Word 67

James Chapter 2 73
James 2:1-7 – Grasping God's Perspective 74
James 2:8-13 – Considering the Two Laws 80
James 2:14-26 – Living by Faith through Works 91

James Chapter 3 106
James 3:1-12 - Taming the Tongue 107
James 3:13-18 – Galvanizing Your Life with Wisdom 119

James Chapter 4 127
James 4:1-10 – Unrolling the Plan for Redemption 138
James 4:11-12 – Submitting to the Ultimate Standard 140
James 4:13-17 – Anchoring Yourself 148

James Chapter 5 156
James 5:1-6 – Shunning Greed 157
James 5:7-12 – Embracing Patience 171
James 5:13-18 – Releasing Life through Community, Relationship and Prayer 184
James 5:19-20 – Pursuing Redemption 196

About the Author 206

Appendix A - Additional Resources to Study James 207

Appendix B - Resources for an Authentic Christian Life 208

Introduction

In June of 2013, I had finished reading a particularly exciting section of *When I Don't Desire God* by John Piper. In that section, Piper conveyed an effective way to memorize whole books of the Bible at a time and I enthusiastically embraced it and began to memorize the Letter of James. It took me longer than I originally planned, but as with many journeys worth taking, arriving at the destination was not the only reward.

After I finished memorizing the last chapter, I felt that God was inspiring me to dedicate whatever time was needed to complete a book about the Letter of James. God introduced to me a desire to dive even deeper into his Word so I can bring back the pearls of truth and mystery he has hidden there. God's gentle strength has guided me throughout the adventure of writing this book and I pray that you will have the same experience as you read it.

The purpose of this book is to inspire and enlighten. Christianity is innately authentic, but people have gotten the terms confused and distorted the meaning. When a person chooses to follow Christ, they are immediately commanded to "Put on the whole armor of God, that you may be able to stand against the schemes of the devil." (Ephesians 6:11) and to "Count it all joy, my brothers, when you meet trials of various kinds…" (James 1:2). These commandments are not for the faint hearted, and that is why Jesus has imparted to us his strength to accomplish them with zeal. When you become a Christian, you are required to become lionhearted and are simultaneously given the strength to achieve it. No matter how long we've been Christians or how much we've read the Bible, we should all be reminded consistently about certain core attributes of Christianity. An authentic Christian lifestyle means that we don't just say we are Christians; we live, think and breathe as Christians.

Authentic Christianity is pursued and embraced through the ideas that are discussed in this book. In this 24/7 war we call life, we must use these concepts to fight under God's authority and treat even the mundane moments as crucial pivot points in a battle. Often we must ignore what seems to be an obvious enemy and instead, attack what lies behind it. As Henry David Thoreau so eloquently put it: "There are a thousand hacking at the branches of evil to one who is striking at the root." In other words, our weapons must be sharp and our aim precise. God's inspiration in the letter of James is a weapon forged in the heart of Christ. Our thoughts must be aligned with our salvation in Christ and our faith raised before us. This is what James was trying to hit home about and that is what we will be exploring.

The author of James, who will be introduced in the first chapter, wrote this book with the inspiration of God. It is a rather unique letter, especially when compared to the letters written by the Apostle Paul. It may seem scattered and a little ADD on the surface. James is constantly jumping from subject to subject without much pause. However, this book is like a beautiful orchestral piece. It flows through many seemingly different sections and notes with gusto. Sometimes it is soft and sweet, and other times it comes to life with a passionate blast of energy. Beyond the surface, there is an underlying current: James desires for everyone to be free from sin and brokenness and to be with Christ. That may sound like too simple of an answer, but God's messages often have a way of boiling down to sweet simplicity.

We are surrounded with opportunities to love things that have no place in God. Our minds are filled with jealously and selfish ambition that causes spiritual sickness and horrible habits (James 3:16). The topics in James' letter are what will keep you afloat in the middle of an ocean of lies. This is not another feel-good sermon; it is a rescue mission for your soul.

Understanding James in Light of the Gospel

Imagine that you're walking around a car dealership just intending to window shop when suddenly you're confronted by a salesman and his large, plastic smile. He excitedly pulls you over to a car near you and says that he's selling it for $1,200 and it's running perfectly. Your interest is piqued because this is the exact car that you've wanted to buy. The paint glistens in the sun and the color calls to you. You slide into the driver's seat and your eyes are greeted by an immaculate interior. The next thing you do is pop the hood of the car to look for rust and damage. No sooner do you look into the hood of the car do you discover a gaping hole where the engine should have been. At this point, how would you feel about the "great deal" that the salesman offered you? How can a vehicle do what it's meant to do without an engine? In that moment, my inclination would be to leave that dealership and never return.

If we are so quick to leave what seemed like a good deal behind because we found that the engine was missing, how can we not do the same thing with our spiritual lives? You cannot drive a car without an engine, and you cannot live as an authentic Christian without the gospel. If we forget the good news of God's mercy and operate from an "I'll do better" mentality, we are missing the gospel altogether and will be forever trying to push our lives along without hope of any power.

James wrote this book to those who already proclaimed acceptance of the gospel, so he does not discuss it explicitly. Because of this, it's possible to read this letter outside of the context of the gospel. Don't let yourself be consumed by guilt or a spirit of legalism while reading though James or this book. We all can naturally commit ourselves to the lost cause of trying to justify ourselves to God by doing good things. The truth is that Jesus has justified us through God, so therefore our works are never about getting on God's good side. We can only be accepted through belief in Jesus' perfect sacrifice and, from there, be able to live like an authentic Christian. From the wrong angle, all of the books of the Bible can have that sickening hue of legalism that can only bring death to your spiritual growth. Do not spoil your good works by laying them on the grave of the law; let them shine out through the grace of God.

Reflection, Prayer and Action

At the end of each section you will have an opportunity to reflect on what you just read, pray that God would help you grab a hold of it, and then take action. Take some time to process through this and answer the questions as honestly as you can. Also, feel free to say the prayer in your own words and add to it to address your current situation. If you have a hard time understanding or applying the ideas in a particular section, consider reading through that section of the letter a few more times. Pray through it and internalize its message before continuing on to the next section.

Before We Start

Please read through the Letter of James at least once before starting this book so you have a high-level, 30,000-foot view of his letter. While I have done my best to capture the revelations that God has given me in this book, I'm still prone to error and misunderstanding. By aligning yourself to the truth of the Word first, you will be able to filter my words through God's words and get the revelation that he intends for you to receive. I would recommend that you keep your Bible open to James and other sections of the Bible that come to mind so that they can be easily referenced. I have often discovered valuable connections between various parts of the Bible by letting myself cross-reference in that way.

JAMES CHAPTER 1

In this chapter, we will see a variety of topics, each seemingly distinct but necessary for the whole picture that James is painting. His writing pallet is filled with reds, blues, yellows and greys and, if we are observant, we can see that he is a master working under the influence of God. From his first greeting to his final exhortation, he is layering and smoothing and expanding the foundation for the rest of the letter. Every topic that is briefly mentioned is revisited later in a stronger light. Every command is reinforced and every joy alluded to again. Being a relatively short letter, James doesn't expound upon most topics in any great detail, but each of the insights he conveys to us are practical and effective.

I find that this first chapter is best read in several smaller chunks as James quickly spreads his canvas wide and, if we go through too quickly, we will think by the end that he is a scatterbrained writer. In order to receive all that God has for us in this letter, we must see the outline clearly before we try to understand any specific topic in clarity. We can glean the most knowledge when we look at the letter as a whole, just as we can be more impacted by an entire painting than just the section in the top left corner.

James 1:1
Pulling Back the Curtain

"James, a servant of God and of the Lord Jesus Christ, To the twelve tribes in the Dispersion: Greetings."
– James 1:1

Who Is James?

The intense practicality of James is evident from the first words laid upon the page. The introduction is quick, effective and to the point, inviting us to play it back in slow motion to see all the intricate detail exhibited in such a short span. James' Spartan, bare bones writing style lends itself to brevity and effectiveness, but regrettably it does have its downsides. For the purposes of this section, the dilemma is this: The author only leaves a slight flourish of a signature before diving into the meat of the letter. However, we can glean some crucial information from this partial fingerprint that will help us better understand this letter.

While there almost certainly were many sides to this author – everyone is much more complex than they may seem on the surface – I'll go over just a few to provide a better perspective for you. I'd like to look at James as a writer, pastor, a servant of God and of Jesus, a brother of Jesus.

Introducing James: The Writer and Pastor

I would consider this facet of James to be the least significant one I'll discuss. What I mean is that God spoke through many personalities over a vast number years to create the Bible, and he never had an issue communicating through any of them. One of the magnificent things about the Bible is that God redeemed corrupt people and ugly events and made something beautiful from them, in the same way that a diamond is made from carbon, heat and pressure, and a rainbow is formed from water droplets and light. If James hadn't been willing to write this letter, God would have delivered it just as magnificently through someone else.

If God was able to inspire anyone to write his words, then why am I commenting on James as a writer? Why can't we just jump into the story and skip the foreword? Well, I have found that a message is always enhanced and brought into focus when I know the messenger. When one of my shy friends, who I know has a difficult time speaking in public, gathers himself up and boldly declares the goodness and mercy of God, I find myself not only awed by the content of his speech but also by the passion in which he speaks, knowing how hard it must have been to break past his shyness.

Knowing the messenger injects the words with a deeper meaning. That is why I desire for us to better understand who James was. His decisive, guillotine-style dispatch of his introduction and greeting is revealing to his character. Throughout his letter, James does not tarry in his delivery of important information. I imagine him like an expert football announcer giving us a detailed play-by-play without missing a beat. Far from being monotone in his delivery, James elevates the truths of God with herculean assertiveness and with joy in his heart. His enthusiasm and passion roar through the pages, but with a zeal that is firmly anchored in reality.

His writing also reveals that he was a poetic prophet. His letter maneuvers within the same vein as the Psalmists, prophets and especially Jesus, in that they utilize many universally relevant events and objects to lay a foundation for higher knowledge in his readers' minds. This style clearly reflects Jesus' own as he spoke in many parables in order to both disguise and reveal the truth to those he spoke to. The practicality and relevance that James' message exudes helps us see what kind of pastor he was.

Being a pastor of the early Church in Jerusalem, his work was at the heart of a fountain of life that God had just burst open through Jesus' death and resurrection. It was James' cheerful pragmatism and willingness to serve that landed him at the forefront of the wave of grace emanating from that fountain. He had a prominent role in the council of Jerusalem in which he and a few others made a decision to not require Gentile converts to be circumcised (Acts 15:13-21). His consistent dedication to scripture is evident in the fact that nearly half of his short speech was a quote from Amos 9:11-12. Also, the authority by which he spoke his suggestion inspired the whole council to come to a consensus and write a letter that would affect Christianity to this day (Acts 15:22-29).

Throughout this letter, James often refers to his audience as "my beloved brothers". The culture of the day was different than ours now, so this phrase was not sexist or partial in any way to males. Rather, he obviously cultivated and fortified a culture of family and closeness within his local church, as well as the greater community of Christians. He certainly meant this letter to be read by more than his immediate church group, so if he interacted with Christians he never met in such a close way, one can only imagine how affectionate he was with those he knew dearly. This of course doesn't mean that he treated anyone as being more valuable in Christ than another (see James 2:1-4 for his abhorrence of partiality), and he exuded a loving, fatherly strength towards all he came in contact with.

Introducing James: The Servant of God and of Jesus

The first sentence of this book sets the foundation and tone for the rest of the letter. It describes a person who has dedicated his life to doing God's will. To fully understand the message, we must see the writing as coming from a deep humility anchored in a profound hope in Christ. By placing no value in himself or his actions on their own, this person does what every Christian is encouraged to do: He filters all his thoughts and actions through God's grace.

As a servant of God, James doesn't pretend that he is the originator of the message that he spoke. He takes on the attitude of a tour guide as he leads us through the caverns of truth and points at all of the goodness, majesty and life found there. At the same time, he kneels down at his readers' feet and humbly offers us the water of life, if only we are willing to accept it. He took a draught of the sweet promises that Jesus presents to us and excitedly passes it on to everyone who will listen.

Introducing James: The Brother of Jesus

There is an interesting paradox in the phrase "James, a servant ... of the Lord Jesus Christ..." (James 1:1). It is believed that James was the biological brother of Jesus from the same mother, Mary. I have two younger brothers and have discovered that sibling rivalry is certainly true. We don't have much documentation that follows Jesus' early life, but one can only imagine that James experienced an array of emotions toward his brother. Don't we all experience moments of confusion, frustration, awe, discomfort and peace in the presence of our perfect God? Imagine growing up with Jesus as your brother and becoming slowly aware that there is something significant in him.

All we know for certain is that James followed Jesus through the entirety of his ministry and became a believer. Here we see James approaching his brother in an incredibly humble way, not only calling himself Jesus' servant, but also calling him Jesus Christ. Contrary to the modern, blasphemous curse, Jesus' last name was not Christ. Rather, Christ was a holy title that was only to be bestowed upon the "Son of David," God's anointed who would rule over the people of God. God promised a descendant to David who would establish God's kingdom forever (2 Samuel 7:12-13, 16). Both genealogies in Matthew chapter 1 and Luke chapter 3 confirm Jesus' descent from David, and Jesus was also referred to many times in Matthew and Mark as being the "Son of David" (Matthew 1:1, 20; 9:27; 12:23; 15:22; 20:30-31; 21:9, 15; 22:42; Mark 10:47-48). We can also see that Jude, Jesus' other brother, follows the same pattern in his letter written around thirteen years after James' letter: "Jude, a servant of Jesus Christ and brother of James..." (Jude 1:1).

Although James and Jude probably referred to themselves as the "brother of Jesus" when they were children, it was not the primary title that they operated under after Jesus' resurrection. Jesus is certainly their brother and our friend, but he must be seen first and foremost as our Lord and we as his servants. If we forget this, we place ourselves above where we ought and skew the relationship that we are meant to have with both Jesus and God. We will be seeing everything as if we are looking through the wrong end of a telescope.

JAMES 1:1

Introducing the Audience: The Scattered Chosen

Now that we know a bit about who James was, let's take a look at the intended readership of the letter. James simply states that his letter is "to the twelve tribes in the Dispersion." The word "dispersion" herein is translated from the Greek word "diaspora", and is translated pretty directly as "scattering." Historians have placed the approximate writing time of this letter between 48 and 62 A.D., making this one of the earliest written books of the New Testament. Only the book of Matthew may have been written earlier, but even that possibility is disputed. Pentecost had already occurred in Jerusalem and Christianity had subsequently flowed out in all directions like a divine invasion of life. Through this greeting, we can infer that one of the primary purposes of this letter was to spiritually unite Christians regardless of when or where they live.

To accomplish this, James wrote for us a collection of challenges, exhortations and warnings. Many of the letters written by the Apostle Paul discuss the process of being saved and accepting grace. This book was explicitly written to Christians, so taking any of James' words out of that context makes them volitile. In the context of salvation and grace, they are life-giving and full of rich, nutritious encouragements and reminders. James' assumption is that his readers have already believed in Jesus as God, and his primary focus is to give a clear understanding on what aspects of our lives to check, how to know when something is wrong, and what to do when that spiritual "check engine" light starts blinking.

While I don't have enough detailed information about James or his audience to fill our mental canvases, I've hopefully given you something like a "connect-the-dots" page that should help you put James' words into focus. In the end, God's revelation to you need not be hindered by limited background information. Now that you've met the author and audience, let me introduce you to the Letter of James.

Reflection, Prayer and Action

- **Reflection**: Where do you feel you're at in your spiritual life, especially when it comes to serving others? Write down some ways that you can start serving God and others better.
- **Prayer**: "God, help me to clearly hear you through the Letter of James. I deeply desire to understand what you have for me to learn and apply to my life. Help me to be your servant and a representative of Jesus to everyone around me."
- **Action**: Schedule some time today to serve someone.

James 1:2-4
Staying on Course

"Consider it a great joy, my brothers, whenever you experience various trials, knowing that the testing of your faith produces endurance. But endurance must do its complete work, so that you may be mature and complete, lacking nothing."
– James 1:2-4 HCSB

"I have not failed. I've just found 10,000 ways that won't work."
– Thomas A. Edison

How Do I Live Like Christ?

After his brief greeting, James plunges into the heart of the question that is answered in many ways throughout this epistle: "How do I live like Christ?" While James covers many topics, he chooses to commence it with encouraging us to be steadfast, even joyfully steadfast in the shadow of chaos.

When I hear the word "steadfastness", excitement isn't the first word that comes to mind. In fact, the words "moss", "glue", and "gum" shuffled into my thoughts when I thought of some synonymous terms. In business, politics, and our personal lives, we are told that refusing to change is a negative trait. During my time in a corporate setting, I have witnessed a startling number of people completely stuck in their ways and causing difficulties for others. I've heard the words, "We've done it like that before" so many times that it is now that all I hear is, "I don't want to do anything different. Can't I just do it my way? I want to be a stick-in-the-mud."

What is meant then by being steadfast through the testing of our faith? Isn't the whole idea of Christianity to grow and mature, constantly changing to adapt to Jesus' resemblance? On the surface it doesn't seem to resemble steadfastness, but we must remember the situation that we are in: Nothing about this change is natural. We cannot do this on our own. We must remain constantly in the presence of God and receive his strength via injection and osmosis. That is the definition of steadfastness. In order to change to become like Jesus, we must go to the only one who is unchanging: God.

Why Should We Be Steadfast?

When I watch football - and I don't often - I always enjoy the plays when a receiver is able to completely shake his coverage and get wide open. Both the quarterback and the receiver's jobs suddenly become much easier and a pass completion is almost certain. The receiver does not suddenly become a better player by being in a good position; the perfect positioning is what enables the player to more easily catch the ball. Now suppose that you see a receiver expertly pull away from all the defensive players. What would you say to that player if he suddenly ran directly towards the players trying to chase him down? If someone were already positioned perfectly, it would be incredibly foolish for him to suddenly alter his game plan.

If a general were to have the advantage in battle, would he surrender the high ground to his enemy without a fight? If a singer were able to hit all her notes perfectly, would she joyfully decide to start singing flatly? If a sailor were secured to his boat, would he purposely hurl himself from safety into the stormy water for no reason? In the same way, if we are anchored in a steadfast love and devotion to Christ, would we want to give that up?

Like it or not, we are standing in the middle of a war zone called life, and if we are to survive, we must hold fast to our faith in Christ. It is crucial that we all open our eyes to the incredible advantage that we have by being in that position. What a joy and relief it is when we are able to shift our perspectives to ensure that God is at the center of our thoughts and actions! "For it has been granted to you that for the sake of Christ you should not only believe in him but also suffer for his sake, engaged in the same conflict that you saw I had and now hear that I still have" (Philippians 1:29-30).

My absolute favorite movie happens to be "The Return of the King". During this third installment of the Lord of the Rings, the city of Gondor is under siege by a massive enemy force that is hell-bent on destroying the city as quickly as possible. At least a dozen siege towers filled with hundreds of combatants have been shoved up to the walls in an attempt to weaken the defenses in preparation for the assault. A grotesque battering ram nicknamed the "Wolf's Head" is then heaved up to the gate and quickly begins to punch a hole in the relatively frail wooden gates that lead directly into the city. Gandalf, a prominent hero in the series, is with a group of fearful soldiers in prime position to defend the entryway to the city. Just as the battering ram is about to make its final swing, Gandalf bellows a command to the men standing by him: "You are soldiers of Gondor! No matter what comes through that gate, you will stand your ground!"

James, having profound insight into the human condition, knew how important it is to encourage us to stand our ground. This first section of James was the perfect way to begin the high-intensity workout of the soul that he was about to embark on with the readers of his letter. I can see him staring us in the face with all of the intensity and sincerity that Gandalf displayed and declaring, "This is not going to be easy. You're going to be harassed by the devil and discouraged by others. You will slip up at some point. You will inevitably discover a lifelong sin that you never addressed that is now a fully-grown, destructive menace in your life. But you are men and women of God! No matter what comes into your life, you will stand your ground! You will receive a reward for this that you cannot even imagine!" We see this thought seconded in 1st Corinthians: "Do you not know that in a race all the runners run, but only one receives the prize? So run that you may obtain it. Every athlete exercises self-control in all things. They do it to receive a perishable wreath, but we an imperishable" (1 Corinthians 9:24-25).

There may be times where placing Jesus at the center may seem to upset other parts of your life. It will disrupt your life and potentially draw the ridicule of others. However, the destruction that this choice causes is entirely good and the ridicule becomes just a fleeting shadow in the light of Jesus' life within you.

JAMES 1:2-4

Steadfast, Not Headstrong

A man named Nicholas and his entire family were woken up around 2 a.m. on July 17th, 1918 and forced to go down to their basement, where they were shot to death by a group of rebels. Upon his death, Nicholas left behind a net worth of about $13.7 billion (in equivalent 2012 U.S. dollars) and the legacy of being the last Tsar of Russia. Even with his twenty-two years on the throne and his unbelievable wealth, his value and title did nothing to help him escape his abrupt end.

One year after he became Tsar, his advisors invited him to consider turning Russia into a democracy. He seems to have openly cringed at the notion that his power would be diluted in any way. On that occasion, he is famously quoted as saying, "…it has come to my knowledge that during the last months there have been heard in some assemblies of the zemstvos [local governments] the voices of those who have indulged in a senseless dream that the zemstvos be called upon to participate in the government of the country. I want everyone to know that I will devote all my strength to maintain, for the good of the whole nation, the principle of absolute autocracy…". During the First World War, the actions of incompetent commanders that he had established lead to the deaths of 3.3 million Russians. His policies during the war also led scores of men away from their farms to fight. Consequently, not enough food was produced and men, women and children starved. Nicholas' decision to preserve his power in the face of change was one of the first of many that would end up bringing him, stunned and wide eyed, to the room where he would be executed. His plan to be absolute ruler ended up being disastrous for Russia and his reign.

In 1917, Nicholas had been forced to abdicate his throne by a government that would shortly become the Soviet Union. This "February Revolution" initiated a complete overhaul of the governmental system. The government that arose from the ashes of Nicholas II's reign eventually invaded and annexed numerous countries over the course of several decades. For many, it appeared that this new government would provide freedom. However, it became obvious to the world over a short period of time that the communist mindset brought with it a heavy price and led to the death of millions more, not only in Russia but in other countries that it annexed. It took over a half century for the Soviet Union to eventually fall, but it was apparent for several decades that the governmental system was destructive and unsustainable. In both of these historical governments we see a lack of flexibility to meet the needs of the people on which the government was based. As any student of history would tell you, this is not the ideal way to stay in power. In 1989, the Soviet Union took one final breath and collapsed in the dust of the Berlin Wall, never to rise again.

What do Nicholas' and the Soviet Union's stories have in common? I would contend that both situations were exacerbated by a reluctance to adjust and adapt. Unwillingness to change has caused countless governments to crumble, businesses to collapse and families to shatter. While a wishy-washy Christianity-ish lifestyle can be spiritually stunting, stubbornness, piety and legalism can be just as crushing. Jesus himself spoke viciously against people who adopt that kind of mindset, saying to them: "You serpents, you brood of vipers, how are you to escape being sentenced to hell?" (Matthew 12:34).

Like a diligent investor, we have to constantly reevaluate our spiritual portfolio to see if we are sinking time and energy into investments that God never intended us to make. The currency of eternity is infinitely more valuable than anything on the stock market, so why would we want to squander any amount of it? Our bodies, minds, wills and emotions are in a constantly fluctuating environment, and careful attention needs to be given to them. By continuing to ask for wisdom, we can maneuver our lives in such a way that maximizes God's life and minimizes headstrong behaviors that accomplish nothing.

The steadfastness that James proposes holds faith with an open hand. This means being willing to admit fault and deeply desiring to seek out the truth. Sometimes we overcomplicate simple things and become so wrapped up in minutia that we no longer see the cross. Other times, we build our own religious traditions that pull us away from our main focus, who is Jesus.

No matter how beautiful you make a padded cell, it is still going to keep you from going anywhere. Sticking proudly with the sinking ship of your own piety is ridiculous when Jesus is right there to rescue. Adopting that kind of "steadfastness", which is really stubborn rebellion, is one of the quickest ways to become a self-righteous killjoy.

The Apostle Paul, whose writings never fail to encourage and exhort his fellow Christians, shines a million-watt beam of light on the path towards Christ-like steadfastness: "Therefore, since we are surrounded by so great a cloud of witnesses, let us also lay aside every weight, and sin which clings so closely, and let us run with endurance the race that is set before us, looking to Jesus, the founder and perfecter of our faith, who for the joy that was set before him endured the cross, despising the shame, and is seated at the right hand of the throne of God" (Hebrews 12:1-2).

How Can I Remain Steadfast?

We often hear something equivalent to this in Christianity: "So then, brothers, stand firm and hold to the traditions that you were taught by us, either by our spoken word or by our letter" (2 Thessalonians 2:15), but for most of us this is no easy task.

I was not born to be a naturally "steadfast" kind of person. While I always remained loyal to the commitments that I made on a certain level, I often flaked out emotionally. When the situation became negative or difficult, I would often cower away without a fight. For those of you who, like me, are not naturally persistent and tenacious in doing good, don't give up! Be zealous for the day that God sees your steadfastness as "being perfect and complete, lacking in nothing" (James 1:4). "Not only that, but we rejoice in our sufferings, knowing that suffering produces endurance, and endurance produces character, and character produces hope, and hope does not put us to shame, because God's love has been poured into our hearts through the Holy Spirit who has been given to us" (Romans 5:3-5).

In the analogy that Paul uses, our Christian life is a race where we must do our best to finish well. This, of course, runs parallel to what James has been conveying in these few verses. So how do we finish well if we do not know how to run? The Holy Spirit is our comforter and guide. In this race, he is our perfect coach. While many coaches use anger to motivate, the Holy Spirit approaches it from a completely different angle. He is at the same time euphorically joyful about how far we have come in our walk with

Christ (even if we have only just become a Christian) and also rapturously impassioned to see us pass the finish line. As C. S. Lewis put it, "Every father is pleased at the baby's first attempt to walk: no father would be satisfied with anything less than a firm, free, manly walk in grown-up son. In the same way, [George MacDonald] said, 'God is easy to please, but hard to satisfy.'"

When I found this quote from John Piper in his book *Future Grace*, I was compelled to add it here as it does an excellent job of explaining how suffering strengthens faith:

> Strange as it may seem, one of the primary purposes of being shaken by suffering is to make our faith more unshakable.
>
> Faith is like muscle tissue: if you stress it to the limit, it gets stronger, not weaker. That's what James means here. When your faith is threatened and tested and stretched to the breaking point, the result is greater capacity to endure.
>
> God loves faith so much that he will test it to the breaking point so as to keep it pure and strong...

God Is in Your Corner

A principal comfort in this struggle to remain steadfast is that God is the primary combatant in the war for your process of perfection. You cannot manufacture your salvation; only God can. How is this a comfort? Think about it this way: God, who is the only constant in a variable world, is your protector. Even if everything melts down around you, you can find comfort in the fact that God hasn't ditched you. In the Bible, this assurance of your salvation because of the rock-solid nature of God is referred to as the "shield of faith". The shield of faith is not an offensive weapon by nature, so when James is speaking of the testing of your faith and steadfastness, he is encouraging you to place all of your trust in God and walk under his protection.

This doesn't imply that you will not need to take action in the process of your perfection. A warrior must point his shield towards the enemy and position himself behind it for it to be effective. We must stay vigilant and never let the enemy out-flank us. For example, imagine that you planted your shield of faith firmly against anger in your life when suddenly you get blindsided by your pride. Would you be ready to direct your faith to this new challenge? Alternatively, imagine that you have started to succeed against your old habit of gossiping. You begin to celebrate this victory but, within a short period of time, you start to see that your celebration in God's work has turned into self-centered pride in your own abilities. Are you ready to apply faith as a shield against your pride that declares, "I am only able to do this because of God"? No matter the situation, we must be ready to apply faith as a shield to every circumstance.

Do you now see how hopeless our situation is without God? We are constantly assaulted in a myriad of ways! However, we will be able to survive and thrive when we call upon God's name and ask him to come alongside us, protect us, and give us advice about how to confront our enemy's next attack. This does not mean that we will become immune to attacks. We are guaranteed that while we are on Earth we will have trouble; we will get knocked down and become wounded. We will feel exhausted and hopeless at times. However, we will always come out on the other end of the battle when God's in our corner. God has designed us to rest in this great comfort, so let's embrace our faith as a shield that will keep us alive. God is in our corner and will bring us out on the other end in victory.

Sharing in the Work of the Saints

A few years ago during Hurricane Sandy, two large trees were ripped out from their roots and flung down into my backyard. One of them broke off a bit of our outdoor swinging bench while the other came smashing down on our deck, obliterating part of it. I opted to do the tree cleanup myself, which would have been a monumental task except that my dad and brothers were kind enough to volunteer. Buying and wielding my own chainsaw felt thoroughly manly and was definitely the highlight of the process. There is something about being able to slice through tough objects like they were butter that brings life to a man's soul. However, as I mentioned these trees were not saplings and hauling around increasingly bulky chunks of wood was challenging work. If I had tried to do it all by myself, I would have certainly felt my frustration and discouragement increase with the size of the wood chunks. Thankfully, I was surrounded by three other men who were working just as heartily as I was. They helped bear my load and brought encouragement to me.

I'm sure that you can probably easily identify the fallen logs and debris that are cluttering your soul. Maybe you're feeling suffocated by the weight of guilt in your life because of what you did to that family member or maybe you can't stop obsessing over whether or not you're going to find or keep a job. Maybe you have been battling a particular sin for years and feel like you keep regressing. Maybe you feel like you're in a spiritual haze where your life is blanketed by confusion. Have you been trying to clear it out all by yourself or are you reaching out for help from other trustworthy and genuine people? Our trials should seldom be encountered on our own. God has placed other Christians in our path through his most glorious invention: the Church. We would be foolish, and maybe even mislead by the devil, if we did not take advantage of this wonderful gift that he has given and allow other Christians to help us through trials.

Not only should others help us, but we should also prepare ourselves to be burden bearers, ready to help someone demolish an obstacle in their life or assist them to hop over it. Frequently, I have found myself on the other side of spiritual funk simply by laying myself and my problems aside and transferring all my energy to someone else. We truly do find life and universal love when we lay down our own desires, and even our lives, for others (John 15:13). Even if someone just gives another a cup of cold water, we know that person "will by no means lose his reward" (Matthew 10:42). When we give, we are bound to hear God saying something similar to what Paul did to Philippi: "Yet it was kind of you to share my trouble" (Philippians 4:14). Please note that helping someone out primarily because you know it will benefit you is inherently selfish and won't bring about lasting results. It is better to simply forget about whether or not something is benefiting us and simply give our full attention to others. The reward is assured, so let us not focus on it. Let's maintain our focus on lightening the burdens of others.

JAMES 1:2-4

Finding Joy in Steadfastness

Another pitfall in our battle for steadfastness is this: We can become joyless in our pursuit of the greatest joy possible. This topic really marries perfectly with the topic we covered on how to remain steadfast. In fact, the joy that God wants to give us in our search for steadfastness is the atomic fuel that propels us into greater love for God and steadfastness in him. James' letter is not about dragging our lives through a dry and dusty existence or a life of complete ease. He wrote this letter so that we could encounter any situation and yet remain completely satisfied and rooted in the reality that supersedes all others.

When someone has myopia, his eyes are only able to take in a small amount of information at any given time, as if staring through a keyhole. However, healthy eyes can take in the full picture and absorb even greater beauty because they are not limited to one point in space. They take in the broken reality we live in as well as the luminous, pulsating beauty of God's reality. Healthy eyes can see the traffic on the road, but they can also enjoy the luscious trees lining the highway. They can see the messy, overgrown lawn and take in the beauty of a dandelion. Dry steadfastness only sees the difficulties; healthy steadfastness takes everything in stride and embraces God in all circumstances. As the Apostle Paul put it, "I know how to be brought low, and I know how to abound. In any and every circumstance, I have learned the secret of facing plenty and hunger, abundance and need. I can do all things through him who strengthens me" (Philippians 4:12-13). Peter also reflects on the deep joys that can occur during and after trials: "In this you rejoice, though now for a little while, if necessary, you have been grieved by various trials, so that the tested genuineness of your faith—more precious than gold that perishes though it is tested by fire—may be found to result in praise and glory and honor at the revelation of Jesus Christ. Though you have not seen him, you love him. Though you do not now see him, you believe in him and rejoice with joy that is inexpressible and filled with glory, obtaining the outcome of your faith, the salvation of your souls" (1 Peter 1:6).

Reflection, Prayer and Action

- **Reflection**: Write down the three areas of your life where you don't feel steadfast. What are some ways you could overcome this? How often do you go to God to pray for more endurance in those areas?
- **Prayer**: "God, help me to be steadfast in you. I want to stay on course with you and need your strength to do so. I know that you're in my corner."
- **Action**: Reach out to someone today who is more steadfast in the areas you identified. Ask them to be praying for you and to keep you accountable as you work on them.

James 1:5-8
Seeking the Wisdom of God

"But if any of you lacks wisdom, let him ask of God, who gives to all generously and without reproach, and it will be given to him. But he must ask in faith without any doubting, for the one who doubts is like the surf of the sea, driven and tossed by the wind. For that man ought not to expect that he will receive anything from the Lord, being a double-minded man, unstable in all his ways."
– James 1:5-8 NASB

"The fool doth think he is wise, but the wise man knows himself to be a fool."
– William Shakespeare, As You Like It

Cannonball

Someone recently showed me a YouTube video of a man in the freezing cold preparing to jump into a backyard pool. The man's breath was steaming in front of him as he drunkenly debated, in another language, with the person taking the video. Once he finally got up the courage, he suddenly catapulted his body from the dock, made himself into a cannonball, and then immediately crashed down on an invisible layer of solid ice that covered the pool without making a dent. While you may not have done something as foolish as that, you have probably faced several situations where everything looked all right on the surface, but when you took the plunge, you hit a solid wall of defeat. Maybe you spent years planning something but ended up hitting a brick wall that appeared too immense to overcome. Maybe you are currently sitting on the dock, unwilling to take a leap of faith into a perfectly defrosted pond because you had a bad experience last time.

James knew humanity only too well. Immediately after James invites us to charge boldly into our new lives, he points us to the tool for sustained endurance: Wisdom. Without God's wisdom, we can easily sprint into a solid wall and spend months or years banging our heads against it without realizing how futile our efforts are. God's wisdom gives us the tools to break down or circumvent the obstacle. In some cases, wisdom will even tell you to rest in front of the problem, even if it is incredibly uncomfortable in that moment.

Accepting God's wisdom means that you no longer let any circumstances drive your decisions or your reactions. This does not mean that you ignore your circumstances, but that their weight in your decision-making process is always trumped by your God-given perspective.

James knew how susceptible people are to the emotions. He knew that we are often driven to take the plunge without gaining wisdom. Without this wisdom, how can be prepared for the adventure? What can we rely on during the journey if truth is not present? James knew that we must be reminded to rely on God, and this reminder is one of the beautiful refrains that he weaves throughout this short letter.

Paul bolsters James' thoughts in Ephesians when he says, "...until we all attain to the unity of the faith and of the knowledge of the Son of God, to mature manhood, to the measure of the stature of the fullness of Christ, so that we may no longer be children, tossed to and fro by the waves and carried about by every wind of doctrine, by human cunning, by craftiness in deceitful schemes. Rather, speaking the truth in love, we are to grow up in every way into him who is the head, into Christ, from whom the whole body, joined and held together by every joint with which it is equipped, when each part is working properly, makes the body grow so that it builds itself up in love." (Eph. 4:13-16).

It Is God's Will That Everyone Ask for Wisdom

In the aerospace industry, it is incredibly important that each aircraft is manufactured with the right parts. Faulty parts have directly caused many airplanes and helicopters to crash, killing or injuring those onboard. Engines, wings, tails, instruments, and even fire extinguishers and batteries have caused numerous catastrophes. One way that the industry has mitigated the risk of faulty parts is to establish rigorous "configuration management" systems to keep track of which parts are being used in which aircraft. By monitoring where each part is coming from and where it's going, a manufacturer can ensure that the aircraft has all the right components. If a supplier finds out that a particular part or batch is defective, it can alert the downstream manufacturers so that they can immediately ground the effected aircraft and replace the dangerous parts with new, safe ones. Replacing one part with another is commonly called "superseding". The older parts are declared unusable and other parts take their place. In the same way, Godly wisdom was designed to supersede – to replace and count as useless and dead – the earthly wisdom that we've been operating under for our entire lives.

I have been immensely encouraged by verse 5 ever since I started memorizing it. To see that God wants everyone to ask for wisdom and to know that if they ask in faith, they will receive it. Everyone! That is a tremendous statement! With this in mind, I have been recommending that everyone ask God for wisdom in finding answers to even basic questions because I know that he will come through on this promise. This applies to those who are currently far from God, are following lies, or are living under a false religion or cult. The wisdom of God can supersede their earthly wisdom in a moment, and so I encourage them to pray for God's wisdom to engulf them. I firmly believe that whoever prays for this wisdom with even the smallest amount of faith will receive lie-exposing, truth-revealing wisdom, and that it will bring about a renewed, God-filled life!

The Truth Is Our Anchor

When James discusses how the "double-minded man is unstable in all his ways," he is referring to any person who, at one time or another, finds himself consciously or unconsciously trying to cram two different paradigms into his head. While it can be easy to flop from one way of thinking to another, that will lead to a loss of direction and focus in the middle of the storms of life.

What I find interesting in verse 6 is that James does not say, "the unwise person is like a wave of the sea driven and tossed by the wind". Instead, he says, "the one who doubts…" That is an astonishing distinction here. In order to receive Godly wisdom, we must first believe. In other words, wisdom is not required in order to believe.

Once we believe, we should immediately ask for wisdom. This is what we are directly instructed to do so in verse 5. Belief is the foundation, but it is not the final destination. Like skilled construction workers, we must establish our spiritual lives upon that foundation in order to see the kind of growth that God desires for us. God never intended us to stick with the same simple notions we have about his character or about our purpose in a childish state of spiritual and natural naivety. However, my metaphor only goes so far. Unlike the foundation of a building, the more wisdom and knowledge we gain, the more our foundational belief is strengthened. This is the beautiful way that our symbiotic spiritual life – "Zoe" – grows. Natural life – "bios" – usually grows by subordinating or consuming other organisms. Zoe is designed to grow simultaneously with other organisms. Rather than absorbing and consuming, it reinforces and enhances. God, in his infinite mercy, has come alongside us in a rescue boat and is offering a way to tether our lives to his through our belief.

Reflection, Prayer and Action

- **Reflection**: Where do you need wisdom now? Have you anchored yourself to God's wisdom? How could you strengthen it more? How often have you asked God for wisdom recently?
- **Prayer**: "God, give me wisdom today. Help me to stay on track with you. I want to follow your directions and do your will, but I need your wisdom to do so."
- **Action**: Schedule times every day this week to pray for God to give you wisdom.

James 1:9-12
Keeping Eternity in Our Sights

"But the brother of humble circumstances is to glory in his high position; and the rich man is to glory in his humiliation, because like flowering grass he will pass away. For the sun rises with a scorching wind and withers the grass; and its flower falls off and the beauty of its appearance is destroyed; so too the rich man in the midst of his pursuits will fade away. Blessed is a man who perseveres under trial; for once he has been approved, he will receive the crown of life which the Lord has promised to those who love Him."
– James 1:9-12 NASB

"Therefore do not throw away your confidence, which has a great reward. For you have need of endurance, so that when you have done the will of God you may receive what is promised."
– Hebrews 10:35-36

Shaping Our Lives

As James talks about poor and rich Christians, he has his sights set on more than current statuses, wealth and actions. He knows that God will be inspecting our lives not as they are now, but as a completed work made up of millions of decisions. Each choice that we make guides our future profoundly. In a way, we are like a potter with a spinning wheel. When he pushes his hands onto a lump of clay, it instantly affects every side. Alternatively, if he just lets the wheel spin without molding the clay, the clay will eventually fly off of the wheel and splatter on the floor. When we make a decision in one part of our lives, it eventually shapes the whole mass of it. If we do not make intentional decisions, the centrifugal force of life's demands will eventually pull us apart.

Some of us may feel that God has given us difficult lives to work with. Maybe your life seems like dry clay that is impossible to sculpt. Maybe your life is like overly wet clay that fluctuates easily and you have difficulty keeping it stable. Maybe you feel like God has flooded you with too many gifts and responsibilities and you'll never be able to grow them all. You may have been born into a poor family, or you may have a natural tendency towards drunkenness, promiscuity or gluttony. What James is saying is that no matter what situation we were born into or have gotten ourselves into, we must substitute his wealth and value for our wealth and value.

How to Be Poor

You'll notice by reading this section that James addresses poor Christians, commending them to "boast in their exaltation". This seems like a bit of an odd recommendation to give to those who are probably working their fingers to the bone just for their daily food. However, we must remember that James is writing this from an eternal perspective. If our lives, filled with difficulty though they are, are only a fraction of our total existence, the rest of our existence must matter the most, right? If we take that thought into the context of the existence of poor Christians here on earth, we can say, "weeping may tarry for the night, but joy comes with the morning" (Psalms 40:5b). While outwardly impoverished, they are inwardly blessed and incredibly rich, both presently and eternally. In fact, James doesn't say anything like, "Everything is horrible now but it'll be better once you go to heaven!" He gives the poor Christian a directive to boast now in the current exulted position that they have in Christ.

Again, James is not speaking of natural exultation in various situations, such as when a person discovers that they bought a winning lottery ticket. There are certainly natural blessings that often come with a belief and trust in Christ. These should be earnestly prayed for and sought after as they glorify God and bring his life into us in numerous ways. Nevertheless, James is primarily speaking of lasting wealth that enables even the poorest of the poor to say that they had been exalted and brought into the place of tremendous wealth because of Christ Jesus.

All who have accepted Christ can turn our eyes from our taxing natural surroundings to our priceless spiritual paradise. This comforting benediction from Paul says it all: "May you be strengthened with all power, according to his glorious might, for all endurance and patience with joy, giving thanks to the Father, who has qualified you to share in the inheritance of the saints in light. He has delivered us from the domain of darkness and transferred us to the kingdom of his beloved Son, in whom we have redemption, the forgiveness of sins." (Colossians 1:11-14). The "inheritance of the saints of light" sounds like an inconceivable windfall!

How to Be Rich

Immediately after giving paradoxical advice to poor Christians on boasting in their exultation, James levels his gaze onto those who God considers to be rich. I'd like to take a second to clarify to whom James is talking in these verses. James chapter five begins with a relatively lengthy – for James – rant against the "rich". He even tells them to "weep and howl for the miseries that are coming" upon them (v. 1). Even though he does not explicitly differentiate what he means by "rich" in each of these portions of his letter, his target audience is not identical in each. The greedy rich people that James tirades against in chapter five are actually a smaller subset of the "rich" within these verses. One can be rich without being greedy. In fact, there are many godly rich persons who give extravagantly and love intensely. James 1:10-11 pertains to the entire population of rich people, regardless of their actions or intentions. Now that I've clarified that, let's take a look at what God wants to say through this verse.

James was not speaking anything against working hard and being diligent, seeking to provide for your family and those who are in need. Instead it is the knowledge that God will bless the hard work that we do and show his kindness to us in this life, but that the ultimate metric - the greatest symbol of wealth - and the most beautiful treasure lies in the crown of life which he has promised to give to those who love him. In the end, this set of scriptures has little to do with money and has everything to do with our belief in eternity.

James encourages all rich people to boast in their "humiliation", as in the absolute reality that they do not truly own anything. The potency of this thought is so intense that many people intentionally or unintentionally deny its veracity and cling to a mind clouded by belongings. To be a Christian is to step away from any childish denial and boast in this immediately humiliating, eternally satisfying truth.

I don't know the last time that you boasted in your humiliation. Often we try to downplay our humiliation to make ourselves feel better, but in the end we can easily feel less valuable by being humiliated. However in this case, James commands the rich to boast in their humiliation. This seems like a strange command coming from anyone, even James. I have spent a lot of time thinking about what James really meant in the particular phrasing that he used. I came to the conclusion that the "humiliation of the rich" does not refer necessarily to the destruction or complete relinquishment of their earthly wealth. Throughout the entire Bible, we see that God blessed many people like Abraham, David and Solomon with natural wealth. Throughout this book I will continue to declare that it is not earthly wealth that is evil, but the love of wealth. "For the love of money is a root of all kinds of evils. It is through this craving that some have wandered away from the faith and pierced themselves with many pangs." (1 Timothy 6:10).

James was referring to the absolute contentment that we can have in God, even though no matter how much money we make or how much we accomplish in this life we will still leave all of it behind. The ideal posture of the rich person is to say to God, "I have all I need in you. You provide for me, so all of my bank accounts, cars and 401(k) are yours. Show me how you want me to interact with your blessings!"

When we truly align our values with God's eternal truth, we gain a righteous compulsion that we must cultivate and encourage. Peter found this and commends us all to achieve it: "Having purified your souls by your obedience to the truth for a sincere brotherly love, love one another earnestly from a pure heart, since you have been born again, not of perishable seed but of imperishable, through the living and abiding word of God; for 'All flesh is like grass and all its glory like the flower of grass. The grass withers, and the flower falls, but the word of the Lord remains forever.' And this word is the good news that was preached to you." (1 Peter 1:22-25).

When we see all humanity as God perceives it, we will agree with the Psalmist who said, "Those of low estate are but a breath; those of high estate are a delusion; in the balances they go up; they are together lighter than a breath" (Psalm 62:9). This statement does not infer the people are of no value, but simply that all status and achievement is in the end "lighter than a breath". David further clarifies this by commending all people to, "Trust in [God] at all times, O people; pour out your heart before him; God is a refuge for us" (Psalm 62:8). Undoubtedly David and James were both intent on steering us away from the hypnotic nature of fame, status and wealth. Instead they are directing us towards the rapturous joy of being eternally free in any temporary circumstance.

Trials and Temptations

No great exposition on eternity like the one that James gives would be complete without referencing trials and difficulties. We naturally (or should I say supernaturally) desire something that this world can never provide for us, putting us in an awkward position of being in constant tension. On top of that, this current reality is not passively holding the tension; it is actively disrupting the pursuit of the joy that we seek. These are the trials that we must face.

When James commends steadfastness under trial, the word "trial" that he uses can be translated as "temptation," or a test of one's integrity. The section after this specifically discusses temptation, but verses 9-12 are not exclusive to temptation. They certainly do help us tackle sinful tendencies, but they also assist us in encountering other types of difficulties. These verses stand at all crossroads in our lives and point us toward God.

Each morning over the past week or so, I have been waking up with a sense that there is an absence of joy in my soul. My mind doesn't know how to make sense of it since everything is going extraordinarily well. My wife is amazing, my baby is growing wonderfully, and I have every reason to be content. I am certainly as contented as I can be in a natural sense, but I know that there are many desires within me that are not satisfied by anything in this world. A divine restlessness has been stirring within me and, though it has been uncomfortable, it is gloriously shaping me into the person that God wants me to be. Since the time I realized what was happening, I have handled this trial in one of two ways: I have either distracted myself from the restlessness in my heart by thinking about something else, or I have fully embraced it and cried out to God for his joy and satisfaction to fill me. The former approach has only left me with a bad aftertaste and a realization that I had missed a rendezvous with God. The latter has felt so simple that it has been mentally revolting. All we must do to find God's blessing is to surrender. All we must do is throw up our hands in surrender to God, asking him to do what we can never accomplish or earn. Failure to surrender is not helped by guilt, and so we have to remind ourselves that we are fully accepted and loved by God, regardless of our performance. Pressing back into God, we can allow ourselves to be completely immersed in the trial of surrender that becomes the trail that leads me to God's presence. When we finally put everything else to the side and run to God, we find indescribable satisfaction in his grace and mercy. The joy that we receive supersedes all perceived difficulty and reluctance to yield. It is at this point in the trial that we receive our great reward: the crown of life.

The Crown of Life

When James describes a part of our reward for encountering trials and living a Christian life, he calls it "the crown of life". The title of our reward alone is enough to give me joy! Just to be clear, I don't believe that James was speaking of a literal crown. When there are no conventional words to convey a message of truth, poetic language may be the only way to awaken the desired response. The implication is simple, yet powerful: "Blessed is the man who makes the Lord his trust..." (Psalm 40:4). It is not our actions in the trial that alone define our victory, but our submissive trust that leads to action (James talks more about this in James chapter 2).

The word for "life" herein is the Greek word "zoe", which is differentiated from biological life by describing a reality and vibrancy that is beyond natural life and originates solely from God. In James 1:12 and in Revelation 2:10, the phrase "the crown of life" alludes to the glory, honor and power found within the life of

Christ that is given to us as a reward for believing, and for acting on that belief. A crown symbolizes authority or victory. While my mind gravitates towards pictures of Disney princess crowns as soon as I hear the word, crowns are not always made of glistening metal. In ancient days, race winners and wrestling champions were given crowns made from woven branches as a sign of their victory. In fact, the word for crown in the Greek is derived from the verb "to weave". In order to make a Greek crown, several branches of a tree or bush were collected and woven together into a beautiful pattern that was strong enough to be worn.

On one level, the metaphor of the crown of life simply means that God's blessings will be placed upon us in heaven. That is indeed a wonderful thing! However, I would contend that there is another powerful story behind this metaphor that God wants to reveal to us. This verse is declaring that God desires to weave our lives into his. Every day that we turn to God, we give him the opportunity to meld his life with ours and draw us closer to him. When we trust in him, he takes our weakness and bolsters it with his strength (Eccl. 4:12). When we realize our utter dependence on God and admit that his grace is sufficient for us, the power of Christ rests upon us (2 Corinthians 12:9). The things that are good in us are being joined with his ultimate goodness and the evil that we finally let go of is pruned away. In the end, our joy is made complete by our glorious dependence and is put on display in the crown of everlasting life. In a sense, we are to become the crown of life.

In all of this, let's not forget one important thing: The beauty of Christianity is that we are not ultimately defined by what we do. As we have seen, steadfastness in the face of adversity is crucial. If we are to survive the freight train of life's worries barreling towards us, we must find our footing somewhere. Certainly our actions are important and we cannot ignore them, but they are merely symptoms we can assess in diagnosing whether we have God's life in us or not. Thankfully, it is who we have put our trust in that truly matters. The crown of life is 100% inherited and given to us on the sole fact that we have thrown our lot in with Jesus and bet all our chips on one thing. This is a majestic crown of faithfulness as heavy as honor and as comforting as mercy.

Reflection, Prayer and Action

- **Reflection**: How have you handled various kinds of situations lately? List a few times where you could have responded with humility in a time of blessing or exultation in a hard environment.
- **Prayer**: "God, help me to look toward the crown of life that you have for me. Help me substitute your wealth and value for my wealth and value."
- **Action**: Take some time each morning this week to cry out to God for his joy and satisfaction to fill you.

JAMES 1:13-15
FORSAKING THE FOOTSTEPS OF DEATH

"Let no one say when he is tempted, 'I am being tempted by God'; for God cannot be tempted by evil, and He Himself does not tempt anyone. But each one is tempted when he is carried away and enticed by his own lust. Then when lust has conceived, it gives birth to sin; and when sin is accomplished, it brings forth death."
– James 1:13-15 NASB

"Temptation comes from our own desires, which entice us and drag us away."
– James 1:14 NLT

"Good and evil both increase at compound interest. That is why the little decisions you and I make every day are of such infinite importance. The smallest good act today is the capture of a strategic point from which, a few months later, you may be able to go on to victories you never dreamed of. An apparently trivial indulgence in lust or anger today is the loss of a ridge or railway line or bridgehead from which the enemy may launch an attack otherwise impossible."
– C.S. Lewis, Mere Christianity

You Will Be Tempted

While it is not initially comforting to hear, the New Testament is saturated with reminders that everyone who follows God will be tempted (Matthew 18:7, 26:41; Luke 22:46; 1 Corinthians 10:13; 1 Thessalonians 3:5; Hebrews 2:18, 4:15). Jesus, who sets the gold standard of holiness for us to follow, spent forty straight days being tempted (Mark 1:13) and continued to be tempted during his time on earth. In one instance, the Holy Spirit actually drove Jesus into the desert to allow him to be tempted, which is a profound example of how the Holy Spirit sometimes interacts with those he loves (Matthew 4:1). God is so deeply interested in our spiritual development that he allows us to go through difficulties and temptations so that we will be faced with situations that will strengthen our character.

Many Christians are surprised by the persistence of temptations in their lives and so are disheartened when they spend months or years battling a certain temptation. While our passions and self-interests are formidable foes to conquer, our God is ready and able to bring us to a new level of freedom on the other side of our temptation. Don't let yourself be discouraged by temptation, but certainly do not underestimate it either.

James only dedicates a few verses to temptation in this part of his letter, but he deals with some crucial aspects of the topic and holds no punches as he describes in vivid language the corrosive nature of succumbing to temptations in our lives.

God Does Not Tempt Anyone with Evil

James has already told us in James 1:2-4 that every Christian will go through trials and difficulties. He said, "Count it all joy when…" not "Count it all joy if…" This means that they are guaranteed to come. If you're not experiencing them now, it's just a matter of time. God will place some of these trails and difficulties in our way in order to strengthen our faith and empower us to experience supernatural joy. Here, we learn that we will also experience temptation while we stand with Christ. That being said, we must be clear that we will never be tempted with evil by God, for James states, "And remember, when you are being tempted, do not say, 'God is tempting me.' God is never tempted to do wrong, and he never tempts anyone else." (James 1:13-14 NLT). We must be wary of conscious or unconscious thoughts that imply that God has placed evil in our path. While it may look like we're splitting hairs, James seemed to believe that there are important implications to whether or not we believe that God tempts people.

Let us compare our findings in James with Jesus' desert experience. In each account of Jesus' time of temptation in the wilderness, we see clearly that God was not involved in the temptation. He certainly positioned Jesus for this trial, but not to promote evil. His intention was to give Jesus the chance to fully depend upon God. However, we see that in each of the devil's attempts to cause Jesus to sin, he used the Word of God. By directly citing verses from the Psalms about God's protection (Psalm 91:11-12) and referencing God's desire to nourish us and bestow his glory on us, he attempts to take the promises of God and disfigure them in order to lead Jesus away from his calling. The devil tried to add poison to truth in an attempt to lure Jesus into sin, and he is still using that approach today. Not only does this approach serve his purpose of drowning us in sin, but it can also attempt to convince us that God is the one tempting us to sin. Thankfully, Jesus did not fall for the enticements and gave us a model life to imitate.

The Rip Current

The variety of ocean beaches is fascinating. Some of them are quite shallow, extending for almost a mile before a massive drop-off, while others quickly slope down into the depths. Some only have bleach-blonde sand while others are mostly covered in razor-sharp seashells. There are even some that, because of their unique topography, cause the incoming water to quickly flow back out to sea in a particular place. This is commonly known as a "rip current". The force of the outgoing water can be substantial and often "rips" people away from the comfortable, shallow water. One minute, a person may be relaxing and floating near shore, and the next he may find himself slip away, frantically fighting against a blitzkrieg of rushing water washing him out to sea. By itself a rip current cannot drown someone, but panic can incite a swimmer to wear himself out, frantically thrashing in an attempt to head straight back to the comfort of the shore. In some cases, swimmers have drowned from exhaustion in these conditions.

As with many of life's solutions, escaping from a rip current is not necessarily intuitive. While drowning people may only think of swimming directly to the shore, experienced swimmers will know that the rip current is much too strong to battle head-on. In order to avoid being pulled out further into the ocean, the unhappy victim must swim perpendicular to the rip current and parallel to the shore. While he is still feeling the pull of the current, he knows that once he is out of the pull of the current, swimming to shore will become substantially easier.

Temptation does not have the power to pull us under, but in the moment it may feel like temptation is the master and we the puppet. Temptation at most only has the power to distort our vision, but not to actually cause us to do anything. Temptation's Achilles heel is exploited by reminding ourselves that our temptation will never be able to drown us unless we let it. The Apostle Paul celebrates this wonderful concept: "No temptation has overtaken you that is not common to man. God is faithful, and he will not let you be tempted beyond your ability, but with the temptation he will also provide the way of escape, that you may be able to endure it" (1 Corinthians 10:13).

As with a rip current, we must not try to directly combat the sin by trying to return to a place of comfort. We also must not become discouraged or anxious when we experience the intensity and duration of sin's pull on us. Instead, we must set our sights on God and follow his lead. Only through God can we reach the shore.

We have probably all experienced the onslaught of temptations in our lives, whether they were related to sex, gambling, lying, gossiping, overeating, mocking, anger, or one of the many other flavors of sin. The topography of our hearts may vary, but each of us has our own rip currents. Each person has his own set of weaknesses and, whether they are socially acceptable or not, they must be dealt with. While some temptations may seem to rise up out of nowhere, I would contend that all of us have a tendency to sin that is bubbling up in our souls waiting for the right moment. Regardless of the types of temptations that we most commonly face, there is a way out!

Jesus never gave in to the temptations that he faced. Instead, he referenced the Word of God in his refusals to the devil's deceptive offers. He looked to God and moved to him rather than focusing solely on the current. Each of the scriptures that Jesus declared during his temptation was from Deuteronomy chapter 6, which starts out with a promise from God: "Now this is the commandment—the statutes and the rules —that the Lord your God commanded me to teach you... that you may fear the Lord your God, you and your son and your son's son, by keeping all his statutes and his commandments, which I command you, all the days of your life, and that your days may be long" (Deuteronomy

6:1-2). Jesus was so convinced that God would fulfill this promise that he resisted everything that tempted him in order to see the promise materialize. He realized God's promise was worth the wait, struggle and pain.

Even when we are alone in every other way, we still have the Father with us. Jesus experienced this in an acute way when he was betrayed in the garden of Gethsemane. All of his closest friends had just fled and his enemies had surrounded him. The full weight of God's wrath had started to pulse down upon him in great tsunamis of fury. We can assume from the narrative that blood vessels in his face had already begun to rupture under the pressure and anticipation of the most painful death imaginable and his brow dripped with anguish. In what would seem like the darkest moment, I'm sure that Jesus was holding fast to the promise that he had prophesied: "Behold, the hour is coming, indeed it has come, when you will be scattered, each to his own home, and will leave me alone. Yet I am not alone, for the Father is with me. I have said these things to you, that in me you may have peace. In the world you will have tribulation. But take heart; I have overcome the world" (John 16:32-33). This declaration was not only a comfort to Jesus in that dark night. This declaration is the pinnacle upon which we must stand when our lives flood with temptation, doubt, and difficulty. We are promised that we will experience temptations, but we are also assured that we can grasp onto courage and stand with Jesus as the sharks surround us. No matter what happens to us physically, emotionally or spiritually, Jesus is there with us. When we clutch this truth to our chest, there is no temptation that can overpower us.

The Pit of Despair

James deals with some of the mechanics of resisting temptation and the devil's works later on in chapter 4:7-10. He placed this short section immediately after the last one to create juxtaposition between the clear fountain of eternal life and the death that sin brings. For now, his focus is on the effects of sin in our lives. What happens when we don't successfully battle sin? Or, to reference James' words, what happens when the sin that was birthed by your desires has been producing death in your life for a long time (James 1:15)? To answer this question, I turn to *The Princess Bride*. This clever movie captured the hearts of everyone in my family long ago and remains one of my favorite movies. While it is essentially a love story, the many classic lines and memorable characters are what have drawn me to watch the movie over and over again.

Westley and Buttercup, the two main characters, fall in love shortly after the film starts and are immediately separated almost before the credits have finished. Westley, the brave protagonist, is presumed murdered by pirates and Buttercup proclaims that she "will never love again." Upon Westley's seemingly miraculous return, he is captured by the evil Prince Humperdinck, knocked unconscious, and wakes up strapped to a wooden table in the "Pit of Despair". The prince's right-hand man subsequently hooks Westley up to "The Machine", which was designed to torture its victims by sucking years of life out of them. Depending on the setting that was applied, between one and fifty years of a person's life could be extracted from them in an excruciating process.

In my mind, "The Machine" serves as a terrifying physical representation of the effect that sin has in our spiritual lives. Whether in one or fifty years, sin desires to consume us and everything that we cherish. Sin, the original parasite, seeks to drown as many souls as it can so that it can breathe in their anger, confusion and despair. It can only flourish in the corruption of God's gifts and bloats itself on the blood of spoilt saints.

Unlike "The Machine", sin often does not bring immediate pain, and the devil has used this to great effect. Sometimes sin draws life from us with little pain, but it is still drawing God's life from us and sooner or later we will feel the loss. You may feel a painful prick when a person sticks you with a needle to draw some blood, but if that person never stops drawing blood from you, you will eventually pass out, go into shock and die. Your body cannot survive with a persistent leak of blood and your soul cannot survive a constant leaching of your spirit by sin.

"The seeds on the rocky soil represent those who hear the message and receive it with joy. But since they don't have deep roots, they believe for a while, then they fall away when they face temptation." (Luke 8:13)

Encountering Freedom from Shame

What do you do when you allow God to break you out of the Pit of Despair and you find yourself breathing clear air? This is an exhilarating experience, but it is usually accompanied by a feeling of deep shame and guilt for having sinned. John Bunyan, in his masterpiece *The Pilgrim's Progress*, provides the perfect metaphor for this feeling:

"This miry slough is such a place as cannot be mended; it is the descent whither the scum and filth that attends conviction for sin doth continually run, and therefore it is called the Slough of Despond; for still, as the sinner is awakened about his lost condition, there ariseth in his soul many fears, and doubts, and discouraging apprehensions, which all of them get together, and settle in this place. And this is the reason of the badness of this ground."

Essentially, Bunyan was saying that once we start to see our sinfulness through Jesus' eyes, we can quickly fall prey to a feeling of despair and filth that is not accompanied by an acknowledgement of Jesus' grace. God desires us to see our own badness and hate it, but not to stay long in that situation. All we need to do is recognize our own desperate situation, call for help, and immediately be saved by his grace. We cannot call if we are not aware that we need saving. As Jesus put it, "Healthy people don't need a doctor—sick people do. I have come to call not those who think they are righteous, but those who know they are sinners." (Mark 2:17 NLT).

A typical bog has these three characteristics: It has limited nutrients, it is toxic, and it is stagnant. This trifecta of negative attributes is what makes bogs a harsh place to live. Few creatures have the stomach for living in such a place. The perfect storm of climate, events and topography has come together to create an environment that cannot sustain most forms of life. It has become a habitat for nothing but bacteria and the occasional bird.

If you look down into your soul, you may find that you are covered in the mire of sin and shame. You may have immediately fallen into despair as soon as you became a Christian because you recognized your sin but have not fully let Jesus mop it up because you are embarrassed or prideful. Maybe you have wallowed around in the swamp of denial about a certain type of sin. This is not where you were meant to live. If you stay, your growth will be stinted and your life will be sapped.

Shame, when not dealt with can have several negative effects. The first is that it can incite us to spiritually starve while being only seconds away from the feast of forgiveness. When we allow ourselves to be dragged away by our desires, we may end up having momentary pleasure but there is a guarantee that if we do not repent and receive forgiveness we will eventually become spiritually gaunt. Just as a natural bog has no food, if we allow sin to lead us, we will find ourselves in a place of desperation and malnutrition in our hearts. At that point, hopelessness may inundate us as we look in every direction and see nothing but muddy water and grey skies. That place is the pit of despair that our hearts gravitate toward. That is the bog of depression that preserves our desire for self-sufficiency while choking our spirit. Thanks to God's mercy, we don't have to stay there! We can be completely free of the pit as soon as we fall into it. His mercy desires to scoop us up and carry us back to the right path. We have no reason to spiritually starve when we are so close to all the life we can possibly crave. But if we stay put, we will die spiritually while being only one step away from victory.

The second effect of not dealing with shame and despair is that they will attempt to work through your life like poison. Even if you were somehow able to find food in a bog, you would still be absorbing toxins that occur naturally. Not only do we experience a lack of wholeness when we neglect to accept forgiveness and grace, but we also experience a sickening in our souls. Not accepting Jesus' forgiveness is at its core an act of disobedience. It is often too easy for me to try to mix God's forgiveness with an act of atonement or sacrifice of my own, as if we need to add to Jesus' works in order to earn our forgiveness. Whenever I realize that I'm doing this, the words of the prophet Samuel echo excitedly in my heart: "Does the LORD take pleasure in burnt offerings and sacrifices as much as in obeying the LORD? Look: to obey is better than sacrifice, to pay attention is better than the fat of rams" (Samuel 15:22 HCSB). If we try to sacrifice in order to pay for our sin, the noxious chemicals of disobedience are released into our veins and we find ourselves choking on our self-righteousness.

Thankfully, we can again avoid this painful situation by relying on God's saving nature. He is naturally and wholeheartedly ready to perform a blood transfusion with us. No matter how many times we fall into the pit, he is standing by and offering his blood to us in the most merciful way.

Lastly (and most subtly), unresolved shame can leave us spiritually stagnant. Another defining characteristic of a bog is that there is little movement. Because of this, toxins build up and nutrients cannot circulate. When a pond or marsh has water flowing from one side to another, flora and fauna stand a much better chance of being healthy and diverse. Lake Wintergreen, which is relatively close to my family's house, is a good example of this. The lake flows from one end to the other; therefore the water is clear, the lake is full of fish, and there are plenty of lily pads and wildlife all around it. On the other hand, there are several other locations where I have seen what happens when the flow of water isn't adequate. The ecosystem in those places was suffocated and everything but the most vigorous plants and animals were choked out, and even the ones that remained weren't flourishing.

Escaping the Slough of Despond

What can you do when you feel that your sin is impossible to escape? The pressure of overcoming the inertia of our sinful nature is a daunting task. In fact, it is impossible for you to do anything about it on your own. If you wait to take Jesus' hand until you are worthy of being pulled from your shame, you will wallow in it forever. If you manage to pull free for a moment, you will quickly fall back into it as soon as you remember your evil. Your best course of action is to remove the disgrace of sin from your life. This starts by fully embracing the idea that you have sinned. Consider how appalling it is that Jesus had to die so that you could be set free. Think about how God had to do this terrible thing so that he could liberate you from the horrendous situation that you were in.

The beauty of mercy is that it is completely undeserved and designed specifically for those who have been broken. If we were worthy of God's mercy, we wouldn't need it. It's not a matter of worthiness, but of acceptance of a free gift. We get to immediately approach God's throne as soon as we sin and ask for forgiveness. This is one of the ways that we keep grace and life flowing in our lives. By accepting an inflowing of God's forgiveness, our hearts can release any toxicity and nutrients can begin to grow in the nooks of our hearts.

But it does not stop there! You must also fully embrace the idea that Jesus has completely cleared you of all blame, sin and dishonor that you have naturally generated. He has done so not because of your goodness, but because of his. By recognizing this, we can avoid trying to earn his deliverance, as if it was some kind of paycheck for your righteous efforts. The only way this works is to recognize our own brokenness. Then, we can simply run from it towards God without thought of how to pay God back. He has given us an extraordinary gift, and we honor him best by just accepting it as humble, spiritually penniless people.

I watched *The Last Action Hero* for the first time about a year into marriage to my wife, Angela. In the movie, Danny, the main character, is magically pulled into a movie with a character played by Arnold Schwarzenegger. At one point, Arnold's character is plunged into a massive, oozing tar pit filled with all kinds of junk. He then bursts out of the tar pit, and within a few seconds all of the tar slides off of him. Danny sees what happened and exclaims, "You know, tar actually sticks to some people." I think Danny's reaction is typical for most of us when we are immediately forgiven and all the tar of our sin and shame falls off us. Everything inside of us screams, "That's crazy! That's not possible! You can't really be free. There must be something that's still stuck to you because you were so deeply immersed in that pit for so long." It is imperative that we realize that no matter how long we were stuck, drowning or reveling in our sin, we can be freed from our shame and guilt immediately and can begin to walk towards a sinless life.

Psalm 40 has been a vital verse for me in my remembrance of God's loyalty and faithfulness. This Psalm is one of King David's songs and starts off like this: "I waited patiently for the Lord; he inclined to me and heard my cry. He drew me up from the pit of destruction, out of the miry bog, and set my feet upon a rock, making my steps secure…" (Psalm 40:1-3).

God's grace glistens magnificently in my life because it gives me the freedom to avoid this suffocating mire of depression and shame in the future. God has spread out a map that we can examine carefully to avoid snares and run hard after his promises. We are no longer flying blindly through life with no idea of what is hurting us or what is growing us. The light of God has broken over the horizon and we can now see the freedom and the captivity that lay in each path we take. Now that we are able to see the possibilities, it is up to us to march toward the correct destination through the proper paths.

In *The Pilgrim's Progress*, we find one of the ways that we can avoid the desperation that comes from being stuck in sin:

> Help's response to Christian's plight is this:
>
> HELP. But why did not you look for the steps?
>
> CHRISTIAN. Fear followed me so hard, that I fled the next way, and fell in.

We must anchor ourselves in God's truth that he loves us and desires that we live a life free from sin. As verse 13 states, "…God cannot be tempted by evil, and he himself tempts no one." God is not pushing our heads underwater to teach us a lesson through our temptations; he is throwing a rescue line to us and all we must do is take a hold of it. "Then the Lord knows how to rescue the godly from trials…" (2 Peter 2:9).

It can be easy for us at times to be filled with fear of one vice and to try to escape it by falling into either despair or into the arms of another vice. Instead, we must press on, not looking to anything but God until we reach his perfection. It will not be easy. In fact, it may at times feel like the hardest path in existence. Pressing on is well worth it. The fight is a good fight and the rest that comes out of it is balm for our tired souls.

Reflection, Prayer and Action

- **Reflection**: How have you been battling temptation lately? Have you been trying to take it head-on or are you looking to God for his help? Or are you allowing temptation to just drag you away into sin?
- **Prayer**: "God, you are perfect and have no sin in you. I need to run to you for help in getting rid of mine. I need your grace and your divine perspective. Give me your eyes to see that my sin is completely washed away."
- **Action**: Take some time today to repent from each specific sin you have been battling with. As you do, picture the sin you've committed just slide off of you, leaving you completely clean. Then thank God for relieving you from guilt and shame so that you can walk in victory away from sin.

JAMES 1:16-18
PARTICIPATING IN GOD'S LIFE

"Do not be deceived, my beloved brothers. Every good gift and every perfect gift is from above, coming down from the Father of lights with whom there is no variation or shadow due to change. Of his own will he brought us forth by the word of truth, that we should be a kind of firstfruits of his creatures."
– James 1:16-18

"Do not be conformed to this world, but be transformed by the renewal of your mind, that by testing you may discern what is the will of God, what is good and acceptable and perfect."
– Romans 12:2

Rejecting the Scams

Several years ago, I heard a story of a teenage girl who, while she was on the highway with her parents', inexplicably opened up the rear passenger door and stepped out of the fast-moving car. Since that time I have heard variations of that tragedy in which she instantly died when she hit the pavement, was hit by another car and broke multiple bones, or survived with just a few scratches. Today, I searched the Internet to see which was true; I found that they were all true. According to the news articles that I saw, there have been many people who have hopped out of cars which were flying down the road.

I wonder what was going on in each of their heads during those moments. They may have been under the influence of drugs or alcohol, didn't realize that they were opening the door, or were just too young to understand the peril of the asphalt zipping by beneath their vehicle. Regardless of their motivation, they were all injured or killed by their mistakes. The highway that was designed to help to them instead became a place of great pain or death. Their deception or distraction became their demise.

While this passage of James flows directly out of the last section, these three verses deserve their own discussion. James has already let us peer into the shadows and is now swiftly bringing us into the light. The storm of uncertainty bubbling up in our hearts at the mention of temptation eating away at us is instantly silenced by the words, "Do not be deceived!" These words are dripping with the same raw authority as when Jesus said, "Peace! Be still!" to the physical storm the disciples encountered (Mark 4:39). God longs for us to see that the storm of temptation can be blown away by the goodness that flows from his nature.

The word "deceived" here is a Greek word meaning to not be led astray and reflects the warning given in verse 14 about being "lured and enticed by our own desires". He immediately follows this thought by saying, "Every good gift and every perfect gift is from above...", emphasizing that not only will our own desires destroy us, but that the alternative brings us every good thing we could possibly need. Our motivation need not be based solely on our running away from bad, but in pursuing good for its own goodness.

The good gifts that Jesus gives to the physically sick and hurting are only shadows of the blessings that he can and does bestow on us spiritually. When we begin to realize that God, the Father of lights, is the only one giving unadulterated beauty, comfort and grace to us, we will sprint to him unswervingly. However, when we allow ourselves to start thinking that we have enough goodness in our lives already, we lull ourselves into a dangerous situation. It is as if we decide that we can jump out of a car on the highway just because we're already going as fast as the other cars. It may seem for a short time that we're doing just fine without God, but it is often not long before we see the consequences of our hazardous predicament. James is speaking directly against this deception that he knows is crouched in our hearts. It is a subtle deception because we can easily fool ourselves into thinking that we are the generators of our own good, when in reality God is the one who has blessed us. I firmly believe that the only momentum that anyone has in his or her life towards goodness is provided to him only by heaven. There is no goodness apart from God, so we must count on God's good gifts to see us through each moment.

Most of us are not at the point where we are letting God's goodness flow through us at every moment. Many times it is due to our short attention spans and difficulty in recognizing patterns in our lives. Most of us can probably go for years and years without seeing the correlation between intentional dependence on God and the blessing that comes from it. At times, I have forgotten to look up and see if I'm standing directly under God's goodness or if I've strayed away. The "greener pastures" that I've found myself in brought short-term happiness but were either a Trojan horse for sin or stunted growth in my life. I thought that I had been allowing God's goodness to flow through me, but in reality I had walked away into an illusion and left all of my blessings behind.

Our deceit is often compounded by our pride, especially when we are certain that we are "good enough" or "not as bad as so-and-so." If we find ourselves nursing this kind of pride in our hearts, we must readopt God's worldview, namely, that none of us are endless mines of goodness. Rather than looking to ourselves to provide good in our lives, we must look to God to fill us. We are all recipients of the grace that comes from God and our goodness is not even our own invention.

Let us not be like Pilate who upon hearing Jesus' words, ignored his authority and decided to show his own "superiority" instead: "Then Pilate said to him, 'So you are a king?' Jesus answered, 'You say that I am a king. For this purpose I was born and for this purpose I have come into the world— to bear witness to the truth. Everyone who is of the truth listens to my voice.' Pilate said to him, 'What is truth?'" (John 18:37-38a). I echo what James says here and I pray that greener pastures, pride, and a desire to manipulate would not deceive us in our search for ultimate goodness.

Distinguishing Good and Evil

James is trying to teach us the primary tactic for evading deceit: To identify what is coming from God, and what is not. Like an expert sniper, James has zeroed in on deceit and is letting us peer through his scope: "Every good gift and every perfect gift is from above, coming down from the Father of lights with whom there is no variation or shadow due to change" (James 1:17). James' words resonate with Jesus' declaration of God's goodness: "If you then, who are evil, know how to give good gifts to your children, how much more will your Father who is in heaven give good things to those who ask him!" (Matthew 7:11).

In the Amplified Bible version of James 1:17 we see James illustrating God's omni-presence and unwavering devotion to his people: "Every good gift and every perfect (free, large, full) gift is from above; it comes down from the Father of all [that gives] light, in [the shining of] Whom there can be no variation [rising or setting] or shadow cast by His turning [as in an eclipse]." God's glory is never concealed from us and, unlike how the sun is occasionally obscured by a solar eclipse, God is never hiding his light from us nor has he ever kept from sharing his light with us. We see consistently over and over in James and the rest of the Bible that God has transferred a massive amount of goodness to our account. The death and resurrection of Christ have given us not only salvation, but also an abundant, incredible windfall of God's goodness. "He did not even spare His own Son but offered Him up for us all; how will He not also with Him grant us everything?" (Romans 8:32 HCSB). God's gift did not stop at the cross; it commenced at the cross and continues to this day in every heart that is being turned to him. What a beautiful, exciting place to be!

God is into all that is good and useful for our daily sanctification, meaning our continued transformation into the representation of Jesus. These good gifts are seen as the antithesis of the temptations "which entice us and drag us away". These good things instead plant us firmly in rich, nutritious spiritual soil and shower us with grace. In this light, the temptations that we are plagued with look like pale, sickly yellow things that have no draw. It is only when we step away from the light do they regain their attraction. Their power is only regained when the ultimate desire of our hearts is absent from our view. We must therefore fix our thoughts and intentions on God and pray earnestly for and fight for a rock-solid relationship with him.

As James has already identified for us several times in this chapter, the good coming from God will probably not be easy all the time. In fact, it may be even more difficult in the short run to handle than if we avoided God completely. Fortunately God's desire to bestow good upon us, problematic as it may seem in the moment, will always be seen in eternity as a blessing. We must determine to stick with it to see our lives turned right side up again.

When we feel ourselves run down with difficulty and hardship in our lives, all we have to do is look back up on the grace that God has shown us in the past and we have the opportunity to echo the words of "Great Is Thy Faithfulness" by Thomas Chisholm:

> Great is Thy faithfulness, O God my Father;
>
> There is no shadow of turning with Thee;
>
> Thou changest not, Thy compassions, they fail not;
>
> As Thou hast been, Thou forever will be.
>
> Great is Thy faithfulness!
>
> Great is Thy faithfulness!
>
> Morning by morning new mercies I see.
>
> All I have needed Thy hand hath provided;
>
> Great is Thy faithfulness, Lord, unto me!

These lyrics run in parallel with Lamentations 3:22-23: "The steadfast love of the LORD never ceases; his mercies never come to an end; they are new every morning; great is your faithfulness." We must actively seek to remind ourselves of the goodness of God and what he has already done in our lives if we are to distinguish good from evil.

Original Creations

In addition to identifying the goodness of God, this section helps answer two questions that I've heard many people ask in one way or another: "How does God view me?" and "What does God want me to become?"

In one real sense, the answer to both of those questions is that God sees us through the lens of Jesus. We are therefore already perfect because of the gift of justification through belief in Jesus. God has chosen to allow Jesus' perfection to absorb the entirety of his wrath so that we can be seen as spotless in his sight. However, we are also not yet perfect in that we still sin and have not yet attained the perfection of Christ in our hearts, which is completed in the process of sanctification through God's grace. Those who have chosen Christ are being daily transformed and renewed through this process. The Holy Spirit steadfastly wills that we should be "…a kind of first fruits of his creatures" (James 1:18). In The Message translation, God is shown to be "showing us off as the crown of all his creatures." He simultaneously sees us as broken, wretched people because of our sin and also as a spotless crown that he delights in. He is showing us off as the most precious of all his creation, symbolized by a golden wreath adorning his head.

If we look back at the verse, we can see the startling reason behind God's choice to make us the crown of all his creatures: God's will. In another epistle, Paul expounds upon this idea: "For all have sinned and fall short of the glory of God, and are justified by his grace as a gift, through the redemption that is in Christ Jesus, whom God put forward as a propitiation by his blood, to be received by faith. This was to show God's righteousness, because in his divine forbearance he had passed over former sins." (Romans 3:23-25 HCSB). God chose to redeem us even though there was nothing redeeming about us. We are made valuable simply because God has picked us up.

As humans, made in the likeness of God and redeemed by Jesus, we are God's most glorious creation, or at least we will end up being so once he is finished with our transformation. He thankfully already sees us as his magnum opus, but we know that he cannot do so without seeing us through the lens of Jesus. His intention is to deluge us with his grace and whisper his love to us until we fully embrace it and open ourselves up to the "Father of lights".

But why does God choose to infuse our lives with his goodness? I answer this question by quoting James 1:18: "Of his own will he brought us forth by the word of truth, that we should be a kind of firstfruits of his creatures." Essentially, his will was to create us. Then, when humanity chose to live contrary to God's best for us, his will is to interrupt our distractedness, knowing what would happen when he did. He knew what we would become. More accurately, he knew who we are at the bedrock of all of our temporary failings and backwardness and chose to redeem us through Jesus' sacrifice.

It is no secret in the Bible that Jesus rejoices over those who grow within the word of truth: "As for what was sown on good soil, this is the one who hears the word and understands it. He indeed bears fruit and yields, in one case a hundredfold, in another sixty, and in another thirty" (Matthew 13:23).

Reflection, Prayer and Action

- **Reflection**: Do you feel like God is a good father? How well do you think you've avoided being deceived?
- **Prayer**: "Heavenly Father, you are wonderful and good! Thank you for the amazing things you've given to me. Keep me from being deceived, especially when it comes to seeing you. I want to delight in you as I should."
- **Action**: Pray this prayer for the next few days, inserting your name as you pray it and speaking it with bold truth: "Do not be deceived, [Your name]. Every good gift and every perfect gift is from above, coming down from the Father of lights with whom there is no variation or shadow due to change. Of his own will he brought [Your name] forth by the word of truth, that [Your name] should be a kind of firstfruits of his creatures." – James 1:16-18

James 1:19-21
Putting on Meekness

"Understand [this], my beloved brethren. Let every man be quick to hear [a ready listener], slow to speak, slow to take offense and to get angry. For man's anger does not promote the righteousness God [wishes and requires]. So get rid of all uncleanness and the rampant outgrowth of wickedness, and in a humble (gentle, modest) spirit receive and welcome the Word which implanted and rooted [in your hearts] contains the power to save your souls."
– James 1:19-21 AMP

"Whoever is slow to anger is better than the mighty, and he who rules his spirit than he who takes a city."
– Proverbs 12:32

Meekness and Righteousness

Now that we have a glimpse God as the holy, majestic Father of lights, James steers us directly onto the path towards meekness and righteousness. This is a fitting direction for James to go. When we know that we have been released from the pull of sin, we can look to God and began to desire his holiness in our lives in an even greater way. In these last few verses James has completely shifted from the depravity of our souls in sin to the righteousness of God that only comes through trusting in Jesus.

Before I go onto the next topic I want to cover, I would like to say that many books have discussed Christ-like meekness and humility in fantastic ways and I am determined to leave that difficult task to them. I will, however, discuss it briefly here for the sake of conveying a clearer picture of what James was saying. If you find that you are interested in the topic of meekness, I'd highly recommend reading *Humility* by Andrew Murray. In a City Church podcast series on the Beatitudes called Glorious Perspective, Justin Kendrick defines meekness as a deep understanding that God is on our side. I also remember hearing someone define meekness as "power under control." I love those descriptions. They give a whole new perspective to Jesus' words: "Blessed are the meek, for they shall inherit the earth" (Matthew 5:5). We see in Jesus' life that meekness is not weakness, even though that is the common interpretation of the word. True, life-giving meekness is acting appropriately and lovingly under the control of the will of God. Jesus was meek when he healed and fed thousands, and he was meek when he passionately drove people out of the temple with a whip because of his love for God (John 2:15-17). All that he did was motivated by a passion for God and done with meekness.

James invites us to take our first step towards meekness by asking three simple things that are impossible to do without Jesus: "...let every person be quick to hear, slow to speak, slow to anger" (James 1:19). Let's divide and mentally conquer these challenges in the following sections.

Quick to Hear

This first topic seems to be easy enough to master on the surface. Aren't we always hearing? I unfortunately have to answer this question in a way that will incriminate most of us. Stephen Covey wrote this humbling exposé of our motivations in his book The *7 Habits of Highly Effective People*: "Most people do not listen with the intent to understand; they listen with the intent to reply." Of course, replying is not in itself a bad thing, but if we are not first seeking to understand, we will most likely miss an opportunity to act in love. I myself am working on this and see it as one of my most outwardly recognizable faults. James believed that God wants us to primarily interact with others in an outwardly focused way. It is all too easy to forget the Holy Spirit's guiding when we are only focused on our own thoughts and not those of others.

I've had the opportunity to give advice to many men over the last few years. I've been able to celebrate with them and provide guidance in areas that I see weakness. My ultimate goal during those times is to hear from the Holy Spirit and simply repeat what I am hearing from him. I pray that this is the case, but unfortunately I know that there have been times where I have recognized a self-absorption and reckless regurgitation of facts and thoughts that resonate with my heart but may have been confusing or even harmful to those I was speaking to. On one occasion I remember postulating on the truth of the certain idea when it suddenly became clear to me that I completely derailed a healthy conversation to air my own knowledge. On another occasion I gave advice to someone that I should have just given to myself. I wanted to satisfy my guilt by projecting my halfhearted desire to be righteous upon someone else. More often than not, what our friends, family members and coworkers need is to be truly heard and not given "facts" or inadequate quick fixes.

What does it mean to truly hear someone or to be truly heard by someone? Leo Buscaglia, a great writer who often delved into the topic of human compassion, gave us a glimpse at what seeking to hear can really do: "Too often we underestimate the power of a touch, a smile, a kind word, a listening ear, an honest compliment, or the smallest act of caring, all of which have the potential to turn a life around". On the same note, Henri Nouwen, a Dutch clergyman, also wrote, "When we honestly ask ourselves which person in our lives means the most to us, we often find that it is those who, instead of giving advice, solutions, or cures, have chosen rather to share our pain and touch our wounds with a warm and tender hand." By intentionally desiring to hear someone, we are displaying God's love to him or her. Whether or not they realize your intentions is not the point; we do not do this for the recognition. We do this because we know that God is watching and is pleased in every step we take, no matter how clumsy, towards humility and meekness in his sight.

Not only should we be quick to hear from others, but also be lightening quick to listen to the words of the Holy Spirit. As our counselor, he has the unique task of providing advice to us every day, moment to moment and, because he is God, he does a superb job. He always knows the best plan of attack or retreat, and he even knows what's going on in the most scrambled parts of us. I know that whenever I have listened to him, I have always come out the other end of any situation having grown and become more fulfilled. Even if it takes a long time, his advice always comes out the winner.

The omniscience of the Holy Spirit, wonderful as it may be, is not forced upon us. We are free to choose to either listen to our own shortsightedness or soak up the words of the expert. He is not responsible for our thick headedness or our refusals to listen. We have this choice because he has given us the ability to choose. Will you choose today to be quick to hear the words of the Holy Spirit?

Slow to Speak

Closely related to the "quick to hear" challenge, being slow to speak brings an additional discovery of our own self-centeredness. If we are quick to hear we are more likely to be slow to speak. These two go hand-in-hand. Like two circles in a Venn diagram, there are areas where these two ideas intersect, and there are areas where being slow to speak expands beyond the scope of being quick to hear.

One area that is obvious to me is the area of gossip. I know that I've been in many cases where I suddenly find myself drawn to share an intimate personal detail about someone that I should not be sharing without their permission. Throughout our culture there's a preposterous amount of evidence that gossip is sweet on the tongue and tantalizing to the ear. Movies, TV shows, books, the news, and our everyday interactions seem to have the sickly hue of gossip overlaid up on them. I will not suggest that fighting gossip is an easy task, but it is an incredibly important fight, even if everything around us says that it's not all that bad.

Another area of being slow to speak is to be careful not to run into giving advice to others. John Steinbeck wrote, "You know how advice is. You only want it if it agrees with what you wanted to do anyway." We are so inundated with advice – even good advice – that it becomes difficult to not just nod politely at it and then throw it in our mental garbage can. Advice is all about quality, not quantity, but sometimes we don't rein in our words. We become like a sweaty, messy lumberjack swinging advice around like a hatchet, thinking that we are being helpful. Many times, the advice that you want to give may need to wait until the right time or place in a relationship with someone. Erma Bombeck made this humorous observation: "When your mother asks, 'Do you want a piece of advice?' it is a mere formality. It doesn't matter if you answer yes or no. You're going to get it anyway." This is not an indictment particularly on mothers, but on every person we know – maybe even ourselves – who seems to be unable to restrain words of advice in the name of being "helpful". As I've mentioned before, advice is not a bad thing. However, it must be given in a way that truly helps. God wants us to primarily interact with others in an outwardly focused way.

Slow to Anger

About a year before Angela and I got married, I was visiting her and her mother who lived about 40 minutes away from me when I realized that it had started to snow pretty heavily. I made the decision to immediately drive home to avoid as much bad weather as possible, thinking that the roads wouldn't be too bad. About a minute into my drive, I had to go down a pretty steep hill in my Subaru Outback Legacy with four-wheel-drive. Unfortunately four-wheel-drive is not useful when trying to slow down or stay in control while heading down a hill. I ended up losing control of the car for a short period of time and almost did a 180 going down the hill. This shook me up pretty badly and my heart was racing for a few minutes afterward. You would expect that I would have been more cautious driving the rest of the way home. For whatever reason, I decided not to drive much more slowly than I normally would even with all of the snow. Driving southbound on 91 seemed to be fine for little while but then I was suddenly out of control of the car again, this time actually sliding so much that the car spun completely around. Thankfully there were no other cars around and I ended up parked nicely in the emergency lane facing the wrong direction on the highway. Again, you would expect that I would've realized that caution was needed, but my adrenaline and everything inside my mind was telling me to get home as soon as possible. About 20 minutes later, I was driving around 35 to 40 miles an hour behind an 18-wheeler when he tapped the brakes. I naturally tapped my brakes, but this normally innocuous act of slowing down slightly caused a chain reaction in which the car ended up sliding off the road and into the ditch off to the side of the fast lane. A flood of frustration, adrenaline, fear and anger rushed over me and I found myself pounding on the steering wheel with all of my might, my face flushed with embarrassment and rage.

The funny thing about adrenaline and fear is that they often cause you to do irrational things that put you into more danger or difficulty than you would otherwise be. The fear that I had allowed to take over my heart and mind was a breeding ground for completely unjustified anger. To quote Yoda: "Fear leads to anger…" Anger seldom comes by itself, but is instead connected with a variety of ailments in our soul. When I was driving in the snow, my chief ailment was founded in distrust in God's faithfulness to take care of me. This schism in my mind and soul promoted one bad decision after another, which generated friction and anger.

James provides an interesting additional thought when he says, "…for the anger of man does not produce the righteousness of God." In the Message translation this passage reads, "God's righteousness doesn't grow from human anger." In other words James is saying that when we plant our lives in the bed of human anger, righteousness doesn't stand a chance of growing there. Does this mean that anger cannot exist in our lives? Yes and no. God-given anger toward corruption, sex trafficking, sadism, masochism, rape, racism, pride, selfishness, violence, oppression, depression, genocide, and all the other works of the devil is justified and necessary to cultivate righteousness. How can we be holy as God is holy if we tolerate sin in any form? In this way, anger must exist in our lives. The difficulty here is that we are prone to fall by the way of human anger when we think we are being righteously angry. To clearly see the difference between righteous anger and human anger, we again look to meekness. The next time you feel anger rise up in you, here is a litmus test to see if it is godly or not: Are your emotions in subjection to God or are you using "righteousness" as a pretext to scorch someone? Remember that Jesus was not afraid to speak out against religious leadership, but we should never think that he did this out of spite or blind rage. When I read the words of Jesus spoken against the religious leaders in Matthew 23, all I hear is love and sadness in his voice. I picture tears rolling down his face as he calls out to them, his voice cracking and aching with sorrow in response to their choice to be separated from him forever.

If the motivation to attain righteousness isn't enough, we also see throughout Scripture other encouragements to be slow to anger. Proverbs, which deals almost entirely with moral situations, is replete with mentions of benefits for being slow to anger. "Whoever is slow to anger is better than the mighty, and he who rules his spirit than he who takes a city" (Proverbs 16:32). "Whoever is slow to anger has great understanding, but he who has a hasty temper exalts folly" (Proverbs 14:29). "A fool gives full vent to his spirit, but a wise man quietly holds it back" (Proverbs 29:11). "A soft answer turns away wrath, but a harsh word stirs up anger" (Proverbs 15:1). And let us not forget the most important facet of all: God is slow to anger and we are called to reflect his nature. "But you, O Lord, are a God merciful and gracious, slow to anger and abounding in steadfast love and faithfulness" (Psalm 86:15).

Implanted and Engrafted

The challenges to be quick to hear, slow to speak, slow to anger are more than just ploys to get us to be nice; they are crucial elements of an environment for the gospel message to grow in our souls. When we realize that James is talking about growing righteousness the same way that a farmer nurtures a seed, the picture becomes a bit clearer.

The first practical way growth occurs is through a heart that is willing to listen. When we're quick to hear, we are receptive to the Word of God and it becomes rooted in our spirits. When we receive the implanted word with meek consciences, it expands into every aspect of our lives. When you're quick to hear, the soil in our minds is quick to accept the good news that God has for us each day, whether it's "new revelation" or a reiteration of something we've heard hundreds of times. More often than not, we simply need to be reminded what we already know. There are some days where I feel incredibly distracted and antsy to the point that I could not function properly for more than 10 minutes at the time. I was biting my nails and having to walk around the floor several times an hour. My mind suddenly decided that the best solution was to get some food to try to satisfy the insatiable wanderlust that I had. Suddenly, I opened up my soul through the help of the Holy Spirit and saw that what I was craving was to embrace Christ at the center of my life with a humble heart. I quickly turned to God and thanked him for the truth that I had been praying over myself.

That made all the difference in the world. The gospel message grows best when constantly received each day by a heart that's willing to admit that it still hasn't got it all yet. The most favorable atmosphere we can create is founded on an understanding of how little we have and how much God has offered. Whenever we look up from ourselves and are quick to hear God's word and the correction and inspiration of others, we are likely to find that we will have a bumper crop of spiritual growth in no time.

The next way this ties into the implanted word is by watering our souls by being helpful and merciful. By reaching beyond ourselves, we open up to the rainclouds of God's blessing in our lives. There's something deeply satisfying about being merciful to others, whether by holding back our speech or by giving a timely word of wisdom to someone in great need. While it can be uncomfortable to hold back from gossiping in the moment, there's a deep cleansing in the soul that comes from holding your tongue. This mercy only makes sense in the light of the received word of God. If we did not receive God's word by being quick to hear, there's no sense in watering our souls. But when we have received his implanted word, hopefulness and mercifulness find their purpose and are instrumental in nurturing that implanted word.

The final way listed in this section to bolster the gospel message in our hearts is to uproot the weeds of anger and fear in our lives by thanking God. Fear and anger create a harsh environment in which anything positive will have a difficult time flourishing. Thanksgiving is the solution; thanksgiving is the weed killer. When we turn our eyes to God and thank him for whatever comes to mind, our hearts expand to receive a fresh rendezvous with the Holy Spirit. Having taking our eyes off of ourselves, the Holy Spirit's job of chucking fear and anger out of our lives becomes much simpler. He is the divine comforter who we can turn to when we, once again, see the toxicity of our souls.

The word "implanted" or "engrafted" herein is a reflection of the same type of word used earlier in verse 15 to describe the conception of sin in our hearts. He draws the parallel between the two situations and challenges us to choose between them. Plainly put, James is inferring that at every moment we are either nurturing a crop of God's word in our hearts or we are neglectfully fostering an infestation of sin. It is true that we are going to sin at times, but we are to do our best to encourage a harvest of life through God's word.

This word for implanting is used not only to describe the conception of a baby, but also in the context of seizing someone or taking someone prisoner. It is the same Greek word that's translated "capture" in Jesus' words in Matthew 26:55: "At that hour Jesus said to the crowds, 'Have you come out as against a robber, with swords and clubs to capture me?'" James' message is clear: Sin naturally flourishes in us, and its main goal is to take us captive.

When I was originally meditating on this part of the text, I ended up discovering something that changed the way that I looked at my interaction with God. In verse 21, James implores us to dispose of certain negative habits and replace them with others. At the time, I received a realization that it is unreasonable to think that we can hold onto wickedness and filthiness and still attain meekness. We only have a certain amount of natural capacity, so to think that we can carry around sin and evil in our lives alongside God's word is foolishness. To receive the implanted word, we must be shedding filthiness, wickedness and evil from our lives. Every bit of his message that we have in us brings us one step closer to looking like Jesus. We have sunk into the depths of the filthy bog and the only thing that will save us is being filled with God's saving grace. As we embrace the message of the cross, our souls become buoyant and we can rise up. I would like to encourage you with a command from Paul: "Do not be conformed to this world, but be transformed by the renewal of your mind, that by testing you may discern what is the will of God, what is good and acceptable and perfect." (Romans 12:2).

Reflection, Prayer and Action

- **Reflection**: What action is hardest for you: Listening, holding your tongue, or only expressing righteous anger? Write down three times you ran into difficulty with that action recently.
- **Prayer**: "God, help me to be quick to hear, slow to speak, and slow to become angry. I want to embrace listening, holding my tongue, and expressing righteous anger when appropriate. Help me to remember that these things will bring me closer to holiness in you."
- **Action**: Now that you've identified what area you are having the most difficulty in, examine what you wrote about it. Take some time to think about ways that you can apply what you learned from this chapter to that area. Write those things down and refer to them often, especially when you're having a hard time.

JAMES 1:22-27
ACTING ON THE WORD

"But prove yourselves doers of the word, and not merely hearers who delude themselves. For if anyone is a hearer of the word and not a doer, he is like a man who looks at his natural face in a mirror; for once he has looked at himself and gone away, he has immediately forgotten what kind of person he was. But one who looks intently at the perfect law, the law of liberty, and abides by it, not having become a forgetful hearer but an effectual doer, this man will be blessed in what he does. If anyone thinks himself to be religious, and yet does not bridle his tongue but deceives his own heart, this man's religion is worthless. Pure and undefiled religion in the sight of our God and Father is this: to visit orphans and widows in their distress, and to keep oneself unstained by the world."
– James 1:22-27 NASB

"For it is not the hearers of the law who are righteous before God, but the doers of the law who will be justified."
– Romans 2:13

Creative Christians

James whips out an intense challenge in this section that he will continue to expound on throughout his letter. He doesn't mince words as he directs our attention to the difference between a person who genuinely follows through with what God has said in comparison with the person who ignores the truth and follows after their own ambitions.

Rick Renner dives into the original language a bit in his book *Sparkling Gems from the Greek* and provides some insight into the phrasing used here: "The word 'doers' is taken from the Greek word *pietes*, the same Greek word used for *a poet*. This word carries with it the idea of *creativity*, such as a poet whose personality includes a creative flair. James is telling us that if we can't easily think of a way to *do* what has been preached to us, we must get creative! We must find ways to *do* the Word."

Paul uses a variation of the Greek word "pietes" in his letter to the Ephesians: "For we are his workmanship [God's creatively fashioned masterpiece] created in Christ Jesus for good works, which God prepared beforehand, that we should walk in them" (Ephesians 2:10). Our Christian lives are not meant to be motivated by a rote schedule of "do this" and "do that"; instead, they are meant to be like a painter's canvas that is progressively filled with creative, inspired flourishes of beautiful actions. Anyone who considers Christianity to be boring is completely mistaken! A Christian's heart is filled, like Jesus', to be poured out in a million expressions of love, compassion and mercy that extend beyond participating in a great worship service and consuming a relevant message on a Sunday morning. When we become doers of the word the way that we are meant to be, we become a volcanic eruption of vivacity and life that sweeps through all barriers and hesitations and pursues actions that will set people free.

Lulled into Complacency

After spending about 15 minutes to read the Letter of James, you may have honed in on the fact that there are many times when James reminds his fellow Christians to not be deceived. In this particular context, he is specifically discussing the relative ease in which we can be lulled into complacency in our knowledge. Some of us may have been able to learn an incredible amount of Scripture and gain knowledge relating to doctrines and theology, but if we don't genuinely pursue action based on that knowledge, we have deceived ourselves into a pseudo-religion that is founded in our knowledge rather than God's mercy. James saw this tendency creeping into his church and probably struggled with it himself. It was vital for him to mention it here again to his broad audience. He is bringing us an awareness of a possible uprising in our minds that could rob us of what we can achieve through Christ.

To solidify this thought in our minds, he draws a comparison between it and a person who is so distracted that he can't even remember what he looks like without a looking in a mirror. The mirrors available in that day were mostly made from polished metal and weren't as crystal clear as today. However, you could still use them to get a good look at yourself through them. It's safe to say that this person James is talking about is in real trouble. He has become so familiar with his routine that he misses out on the details. As with all learning, gaining knowledge of Christ takes time and focus to ensure that we are getting all the facts straight. Where it deviates from regular learning is that it cannot be really attained without being filtered through Christ in us. In other words, the revelation of God can only be attained when we allow for Christ to call the shots. This is more than just academic, mental ascension to knowledge of God; it is a journey to captivate our own hearts with God.

On top of having to constantly rewire our natural tendencies, we have to be aware of the spiritual forces that seek to spin us into confusion. We are being bombarded with distractions every day. The myriad of interruptions will eat away at our focus if we're not careful. Each barrage is strategic and filled with deadly intent, which doesn't bode well when we are not intentionally guiding our hearts toward Jesus.

Whether unjustified contentment without action can be attributed to our circumstances, our own deception, or both, we are under orders to fight this deception and cling tightly to the action that God has called us to with his scriptures. Let it be said of us that we consistently look into the perfect law of liberty.

Pure Religion

Now that we have established that our knowledge calls us to action, we must pass our actions through this acid test: "Do my words and actions reflect the priorities of Christ?" This question is imperative to finding out whether or not our religion is "pure and undefiled". C.S. Lewis expertly deals with the topic of pure religion on his book *The Screwtape Letters*. This fictional book is comprised of letters sent from a senior demon, Screwtape, to a junior tempter demon named Wormwood. In one letter, Screwtape provides some diabolical advice on curdling the religion in human souls: "The real trouble about the set your patient is living in is that it is *merely* Christian... What we want, if men become Christians at all, is to keep them in the state of mind I call 'Christianity And'. You know — Christianity and the Crisis, Christianity and the New Psychology, Christianity and the New Order, Christianity and Faith Healing, Christianity and Psychical Research, Christianity and Vegetarianism, Christianity and Spelling Reform. If they must be Christians let them at least be Christians with a difference. Substitute for the faith itself some Fashion with a Christian colouring."

When we read in this section of James' letter about a "religion that is pure and undefiled", we must know that James was not speaking about a kind of Christianity that puts anything on the same level as our relationship and service to Christ. If we place politics, sports, hobbies, news, entertainment, scandal and gossip within the same ring of influence and supremacy as God, we begin to grow curdled religion in our hearts. Becoming a Christian means that we adjust our perspective towards everything that we do and believe. We need to take a few steps back, analyze our hearts, and be willing to sacrifice some of the things that we held so dearly because they don't line up with the truth of the cross. This does not mean that your personality and uniqueness will be lost, or that you will become a drone-like, self-sacrificing doormat. It means that when you sacrifice your energy, position, time and even your life, you have the opportunity to become a richer, more substantive, more complete version of yourself than you can imagined.

The compassion and mercy in our hearts must extend to those who are in need. Those who are truly internalizing God's word and responding with action are those who are pouring their lives out in the pursuit of those in need. James specifically points out the widows and orphans in his statement because they were the poorest types of people in that day (and many are still today). James is saying, "If your heart really grabs a hold of the gospel, you're going to be inspired to jump in situations where you can help those in deep need."

Reflection, Prayer and Action

- **Reflection**: Do you feel like you've been a creative doer of God's word? Or have you been lulled into complacency? What thoughts about your actions popped into your head while you were reading this chapter?
- **Prayer**: "God, help me to apply your word to my life with creativity and zeal! Let me always seek to put your word and desires above mine. I know that this is the best, most ultimately satisfying way I could live my life."
- **Action**: You pick the action this time. Ask God how he wants you to apply his word to your life and do it.

James Chapter 2

This chapter contains only three major topics, whereas Chapter 1 has eight. This enables James to deal with each of them in more comprehensive ways in Chapter 2. He begins with an exposition on the human heart in the context of God's perspective and shows us how radically we have missed the mark. He then leverages this closer understanding of the topic of partiality to show the effect our sin has upon the law.

He wraps up the chapter with a section regarding faith and actions. He spends more time on that topic than any other in his letter because it is such a delicate and vital idea. It is delicate because it can be so easily misunderstood if not taken fully in context and it is vital because it affects how Christians respond to salvation and belief.

JAMES 2:1-7
GRASPING GOD'S PERSPECTIVE

"My brothers, show no partiality as you hold the faith in our Lord Jesus Christ, the Lord of glory. For if a man wearing a gold ring and fine clothing comes into your assembly, and a poor man in shabby clothing also comes in, and if you pay attention to the one who wears the fine clothing and say, 'You sit here in a good place,' while you say to the poor man, 'You stand over there,' or, 'Sit down at my feet,' have you not then made distinctions among yourselves and become judges with evil thoughts? Listen, my beloved brothers, has not God chosen those who are poor in the world to be rich in faith and heirs of the kingdom, which he has promised to those who love him? But you have dishonored the poor man. Are not the rich the ones who oppress you, and the ones who drag you into court? Are they not the ones who blaspheme the honorable name by which you were called?"
– James 2:1-7

"There will be tribulation and distress for every human being who does evil, the Jew first and also the Greek, but glory and honor and peace for everyone who does good, the Jew first and also the Greek. For God shows no partiality."
– Romans 2:9-11

Getting Ahead

The New York Auto Show was a big hit with my family for a few years. We would pack into the Suburban and Dad would drive us all down to the Big Apple for a day of cool displays and exquisite cars. This annual event brings together hundreds of automakers from around the world, each with the desire to sell as many cars as possible. The basic intention of each manufacturer's presence is to draw in as many enthusiasts, wealthy persons, and car magazine writers as possible to get the word out about their newest car models.

After finding a parking spot somewhere a few blocks away, we would make our way to the Jacob Javits Center and into a world of automobiles. I usually wanted to skim right over the displays for Jeeps, SUVs and vans and move on to the sports cars. The hotrod reds and metallic blues drew me in and I couldn't help getting excited about sitting in all of them. Now there is absolutely nothing wrong with an SUV or van, but there's a racecar driver inside of me waiting to turn on the ignition, hear the car roar, and peel out in a blaze of glory. I realized after that day that I reacted to the different vehicles in fundamentally different ways because I saw much more value in one than the other. I could get much more use out of an SUV, and a Honda Civic gets better gas mileage, but my mind was drawn to the glitz, extravagance and authority of the absurdly powerful 900+ horsepower machines.

My concern here is that if we are not careful, we can find ourselves treating some people like Ferraris and others like minivans because we see more apparent worth in some than others. When interacting with a boss, homeless person, famous musician, spouse, or grocery clerk, you can naturally fall into a dangerous position of looking at certain people as less or more valuable than others. I don't believe that this means that we should treat everyone exactly the same. Clearly, we should treat our spouses differently than our bosses and our leaders differently than our children. That is a given. However, I do mean that we should never see anyone as being less or more valuable to God than another person.

There are several reasons for this biased, preferential treatment towards some people and coldness towards others:

Firstly, culture has set for us a variety of standard protocols for interacting with people. Some are morally neutral, like shaking someone's hand, while many others are morally positive, like holding the door open for a pregnant woman or someone in a wheel chair. We are most definitely called to direct our efforts towards those who need it most. We should also not neglect those who only moderately need our help. While these actions are often attributed to a sort of resurrected "chivalry", they really are just Christian values that are exhibited in everyday actions, whether or not people realize it. The danger is that this approach relies heavily on how we perceive people rather than upon their actual needs.

For example, being a man I don't feel any special social obligation to hold the door open for another man. However, my little bit of kindness towards my fellow man may change the course of his life. I am not omniscient regarding the effects of my actions and therefore should always treat every chance to be kind to others as a golden opportunity. In other words, our standard social protocols must be bolstered by Holy Spirit-directed kindness towards everyone, whether or not we think that they're in need.

Secondly – and this is the more deadly reason – we may consciously or unconsciously interact with people based on what they can offer us. This seems to be what James is zeroing in on when he uses a rich man and a poor man in his example. James reminds us that "if you pay attention to the one who wears the fine clothing [the affluent person]...have you not then made distinctions among yourselves and become judges with evil thoughts?" (James 2:3-4). It is all too easy to treat those who appear to have authority to increase personal gain with a smarmy "super-kindness" that comes straight from self-interest and accomplishes nothing in God's eyes. James was clever in the way that he wrote this first thought. He directly calls one man "poor" while he describes the other man as "wearing a gold ring and fine clothing." This category not only includes those who are rich and powerful, but also those who are charlatans who go around pretending to be so. Those of us with sports cars, houses, suits, dozens of shoes and expensive jewelry may fall within this category. We seek to deceive others into catering to us by manufacturing our own false importance.

The irony of all of this is that by deferring to those who are "in power" sometimes means that we are giving more power to those who are already hurting the Christians and their message. Eugene Peterson translates James 2:5-7 this way: "Listen, dear friends. Isn't it clear by now that God operates quite differently? He chose the world's down-and-out as the kingdom's first citizens, with full rights and privileges. This kingdom is promised to anyone who loves God. And here you are abusing these same citizens! Isn't it the high and mighty who exploit you, who use the courts to rob you blind? Aren't they the ones who scorn the new name—'Christian'—used in your baptisms?" (James 2:5-7 MSG).

This group of deceivers doesn't just include the "fake" rich; it can also include people who are pretending to be spiritually important. Have we ever tried to throw ourselves vigorously into this category on occasion because we wanted to be seen as spiritually elite (whatever that really means) to impress others? Have we puffed ourselves up in the "fine clothing" of arrogant spirituality and bragging? Have we worn the "gold ring" of false humility and name-dropping?

If we are not careful, we will end up sitting on a throne of our own "righteousness" that has its foundation in sin. Our own righteousness is a shifting, unreliable thing that is treacherous and even is prone to judging God for his impartial justice. "Shall one who hates justice govern? Will you condemn him who is righteous and mighty, who says to a king, 'Worthless one,' and to nobles, 'Wicked man,' who shows no partiality to princes, nor regards the rich more than the poor, for they are all the work of his hands?" (Job 34:17-19).

Whether immediately, down the road, or in the next life, these selfish actions directed towards those who seem important will ensnare their creators. The "cleverness" of the selfish will be their undoing. This sin of self-centeredness will not go unnoticed by God. As Paul said in his letter to Colossae, "For the wrongdoer will be paid back for the wrong he has done, and there is no partiality" (Colossians 3:25).

Let us always find our footing in loving Christ and others. Jesus has rescued us from sin; however, the full impact of the rescue from sin starts when we pull out of selfishness and self-concern. When that happens, we are freed to find refuge and satisfaction in vibrant, whole-hearted love that always seeks the good of others.

Reflection, Prayer and Action

- **Reflection**: How do you view people? When you're honest with yourself, do you interact with people mainly because of the benefits they can give you, or because they're valuable to God?
- **Prayer**: "God, help me to see people the way you see them. Give me the grace to avoid cultural pitfalls and selfishness as I bless others because you first blessed me."
- **Action**: Talk to some people in your workplace or school that you haven't talked to before or haven't talked to in a while. Before you do, pray that God will help you to see them as he does.

James 2:8-13
Considering the Two Laws

"If, however, you are fulfilling the royal law according to the Scripture, 'You shall love your neighbor as yourself,' you are doing well. But if you show partiality, you are committing sin and are convicted by the law as transgressors. For whoever keeps the whole law and yet stumbles in one point, he has become guilty of all. For He who said, 'Do not commit adultery,' also said, 'Do not commit murder.' Now if you do not commit adultery, but do commit murder, you have become a transgressor of the law. So speak and so act as those who are to be judged by the law of liberty. For judgment will be merciless to one who has shown no mercy; mercy triumphs over judgment."
– James 2:8-13 NASB

"Hear, O Israel: The Lord our God, the Lord is one. You shall love the Lord your God with all your heart and with all your soul and with all your might."
– Deuteronomy 6:4-5

The Stained Glass Law

In his commentary on James in his *ESV Study Bible*, James MacArthur describes God's law as being a single piece of glass. When I imagine what that piece of glass would look like, I see it as a beautiful, stained glass portrait of God in all of his blazing righteousness. I know that a stained glass window does not behave in the same way as a single pane of glass, but please indulge my imagination. I then envision that my selfishness in one instance is like a spiritual sledgehammer that has been hurled at the section of the portrait representing God's requirement to be unselfish. What do you see happening next? In my mind, the window is rocked by the force of the blow in that one section. The entire masterpiece then splinters into countless fragments that come crashing down on the floor. That single blow to one part of the portrait reverberated throughout the stained glass. MacArthur uses the analogy of the sheet of glass to represent God's law because, he says, by breaking a part of the law you have broken the integrity of the whole law. It is not that my one sin caused me to commit every other sin under the law, but that my selfishness obliterated the flawlessness of the law that I am required to keep. For me, it is no longer structurally sound and does not carry the perfection that God righteously demands. Unfortunately, from when we were young children, we have been continually smashing the glass of the law, often repeating the same sin over and over.

But doesn't this analogy make it seem as though all sins are equally devastating, from lying to murder? How is it fair to compare two sins that seem so vastly different to us? Where this question goes wrong is that it assumes that God lives on the same moral plane as us. Culturally or mentally, we have learned that certain social behaviors may not be deemed so "bad" or at least not as bad as some other sins we have heard about. Unfortunately for our human nature, there are not certain tiers of sins that are seen as less evil than others. For example, the sin of homosexuality somehow has been deemed, by many Christians, to be the most extreme sin, while fornication (sex outside of marriage) doesn't elicit the nearly the same outrage from Christian communities. I am not trying to argue to what extent particular sins have damaged our society and culture. I simply desire to urgently point our attention to God's opinion and show that all sins, no matter how frowned upon or celebrated by our society, are equally disruptive to our perfection in Christ. When we take a sledgehammer of lust, greed or anger to one part of the law, its entire purity is violated. Like Humpty Dumpty, we cannot simply glue back all of the pieces and expect the glass to do what it was meant to do. All of your "goodness" and all of your mending cannot put the law back together again. Once it is broken even once, there is nothing on earth that can repair it.

Do not think that I am speaking evil against the law. We see in Romans that the law is not at fault by any means: "What should we say then? Is the law sin? Absolutely not! On the contrary, I would not have known sin if it were not for the law. For example, I would not have known what it is to covet if the law had not said, Do not covet" (Romans 7:7 HCSB). So we see that the law is all goodness, but to us who were born in spiritual poverty its nourishment lies beneath a barrier that cannot be penetrated by our imperfection. As MacArthur put it, "The law diagnoses the problem but does nothing to treat it." It was designed to be acted out by and fulfilled by one perfect person. We cannot ever be truly good before God, even if we think we're blameless: "If I sin, what do I do to you, you watcher of mankind? Why have you made me your mark? Why have I become a burden to you? Why do you not pardon my transgression and take away my iniquity? For now I shall lie in the earth; you will seek me, but I shall not be" (Job 7:20-21). If we are trying to become satisfied by the law alone, we are like hungry children standing empty-handed in front of a vending machine, hoping that bags of chips and cookies will start automatically dispensing to us. We don't have the currency to reach the nourishment. That is where God's complete forgiveness comes into play. Thank God that anyone who believes in Christ can see that glass completely restored through forgiveness and receive, through the currency of faith, the satisfaction and life that is hidden in it. Jesus was the perfect person who fulfilled the law and is now living inside of those who believe to enable us to walk blamelessly, no matter how much we previously obliterated the law.

Of course, in talking about complete forgiveness for all sin, I must mention the sin that has been called the "eternal sin". This sin, committed against the law, is mentioned in Mark 3:22-30 and Matthew 12:31-32 where Jesus declared that blasphemy against the Holy Spirit would never be forgiven. On the surface, this seems to be a contradiction to Jesus' previous statements on the power and universality of forgiveness for those who seek it. This statement has been interpreted in various ways, but Jesus was talking about the sin of definitive rejection of the Holy Spirit's work of salvation through Jesus. When restated in that way, it becomes easier to understand in light of all of Jesus' teachings. To summarize, all who seek forgiveness will find it. The only ones who will not receive forgiveness are those who will entirely reject the one who offers the only forgiveness available. I do not believe that the eternal sin can ever apply to those of us who believe in Jesus and desire God in our lives. God has an entirely seamless, perfect track record to bestow upon anyone who receives Jesus as Lord, so let us run to Jesus for forgiveness!

The Law of Liberty

While Jesus fulfilled the original law for us, it is the law of liberty that truly carries us through the gates of victory and onto greater things than simply being pulled up from the destruction of the old law. By suddenly saying, "So speak and so act as those who are to be judged under the law of liberty", it appears that James has thrown a bowling ball that obliterates everything he has already said about the law. If this "law of liberty" stands to free us from the law that is so fragile and impossible to keep, what is the point in the original law? If we are all under the law of liberty, doesn't this mean that we are now free to do whatever we please? By no means! Jesus clearly stated that he did not come to do away with the law, but to fulfill it. By fulfilling the law through his sacrificial life and death, Jesus has divinely un-shattered the law that we have spent our lives intentionally or unconsciously smashing. By this miracle, we are no longer held by the noose of our sin and we have become free under the law of liberty.

Now, there is a nuance here that I have found hard to explain and I hope that I do not mislead you one way or another. The two laws are notoriously difficult for our crooked nature to comprehend. To best explain this, I have pulled this chunk of scripture from Galatians that reveals the heart of God concerning this topic. I hope you'll see the strong, reinforcing parallels between these sections of James and Galatians: "For you were called to freedom, brothers. Only do not use your freedom as an opportunity for the flesh, but through love serve one another. For the whole law is fulfilled in one word: 'You shall love your neighbor as yourself.' But if you bite and devour one another, watch out that you are not consumed by one another. But I say, walk by the Spirit, and you will not gratify the desires of the flesh. For the desires of the flesh are against the Spirit, and the desires of the Spirit are against the flesh, for these are opposed to each other, to keep you from doing the things you want to do. But if you are led by the Spirit, you are not under the law. Now the works of the flesh are evident: sexual immorality, impurity, sensuality, idolatry, sorcery, enmity, strife, jealousy, fits of anger, rivalries, dissensions, divisions, envy, drunkenness, orgies, and things like these. I warn you, as I warned you before, that those who do such things will not inherit the kingdom of God. But the fruit of the Spirit is love, joy, peace, patience, kindness, goodness, faithfulness, gentleness, self-control; against such things there is no law. And those who belong to Christ Jesus have crucified the flesh with its passions and desires. If we live by the Spirit, let us also keep in step with the Spirit. Let us not become conceited, provoking one another, envying one another" (Gal. 5:13-26).

Hopefully you have gotten a sense of the divine tension between freedom and serving in this passage. Since we are to be judged under the law of liberty, we must have a firm grasp on the concept of both being completely free while still being, in a beautiful sense, bound to others as servants. The freedom we are called to, rather than being the cultural battle cry of self-interest, is to be directed at those whom we can serve.

Another aspect of the law of liberty is that anyone functioning under it must be led by Holy Spirit. In other words, you can only obey the law of liberty by being under the direction of the Holy Spirit. Far from letting us do whatever we want, the law of liberty requires us to be in lockstep with the Holy Spirit. The law of liberty does not focus primarily on avoiding bad things and doing good things. It is infatuated with obeying God by doing the exact thing that God desires us to do in each moment. In writing this, I am reminded of Romans 14:23b that says, "For whatever does not proceed from faith is sin." This sobering phrase not only blows our righteousness out of the water but also shows us how closely we must be in step with the Holy Spirit in faith. We can sacrifice, help others, and be generous, but if we are disobeying the Holy Spirit in the process, our actions are become sinful because we have not placed God's will over our own.

Thankfully, there is grace in this department for all of us, but it is better for our souls if we obey rather than trespass upon God's grace by our defiance, laziness or deafness. What the Holy Spirit desires you to do will always end up being the most joyful and pleasurable path you can take. Disobedience always ends in disillusionment and pain.

Mercy Received, Mercy Given

In this section, James makes it clear that a person who does not give mercy will not receive it. On the surface, we see that this is because God demands that we give mercy to others, for he said, "You shall not take vengeance or bear a grudge against the sons of your own people, but you shall love your neighbor as yourself: I am the Lord" (Leviticus 19:18). We also see in 1 John that if we show contempt for our fellow man, we are convicted under charges of not really loving God: "If anyone says, I love God, and hates (detests, abominates) his brother [in Christ], he is a liar; for he who does not love his brother, whom he has seen, cannot love God, Whom he has not seen. And this command (charge, order, injunction) we have from Him: that he who loves God shall love his brother [believer] also" (1 John 4:20-21 AMP). Now, it is good for us to understand that we are required to give mercy to others, but if we stop at that thought we will miss out on the heart of the gospel.

After reading James 1:13 many times, I still thought that James was saying that we had to earn mercy by giving it to others. Our minds naturally respond in disbelief and misunderstanding when we hear about gifts with no strings attached. What I failed to see is the fatal flaw in my viewpoint: We do not have the capacity on our own to give mercy, so how can we ever give enough to receive it? I realized that I had to shift my perspective to see the foundation upon which this verse was built. What I had missed was this: The mercy given to us by Jesus is the only antidote available. Many of us try to cover up our condition and dish out human mercy, only to find that even though we may have fooled others, we will never be able to fool ourselves or God. There is a secret, festering sickness in each person who has not received the mercy that comes from God, and that sickness precludes us from giving out any genuinely divine mercy.

I eventually discovered that for mercy to be true mercy, it must be given without payment or subsidy, meaning that this mercy that James was mentioning had to have its source in Jesus. I had missed the key to all of this, which is that God must first show mercy to us freely before we can pass it onto others. If we refuse his mercy and run away from it, we will never be able to give mercy to others.

God's mercy was not meant to be locked up or hidden in our hearts.

Judgment without mercy rests solely on those who reject God's personal mercy for them. Some of these people are included in the list of those who have or will commit the eternal sin that Jesus warned against. However, a great many current Christians (and future Christians) are still in the process of letting God's mercy into their lives, whether they realize it or not. Many of these people praise mercy and speak highly of it in theory, but have a difficult time being compassionate or forgiving to others.

Once anyone gets a taste of divine mercy and discovers that it comes from a never-ending source, there is most often a spiritual renaissance that embraces a desire for more mercy. True mercy "rejoiceth against judgment" (James 2:13 KJV), meaning that the very nature of mercy creates a joyful party in our hearts that overflows upon others. It an experience of mercy that led Peter to remind the Jerusalem Council that we all need a substantial dose of grace to be free from the yoke of perfection that no one can bear: "Now, therefore, why are you putting God to the test by placing a yoke on the neck of the disciples that neither our fathers nor we have been able to bear? But we believe that we will be saved through the grace of the Lord Jesus, just as they will" (Acts 15:10). It was the perfect knowledge of mercy that led Jesus to rebuke the religious leaders for their refusal to distribute mercy: "Woe to you, scribes and Pharisees, hypocrites! For you tithe mint and dill and cumin, and have neglected the weightier matters of the law: justice and mercy and faithfulness. These you ought to have done, without neglecting the others" (Matthew 23:23). According to Jesus' death and resurrection, we now live in an era where mercy is standing over the grave of judgment with a triumphant roar, desiring that no one ever experience judgment in the absence of grace. That same triumphant roar can be ours. When we allow God's mercy to enter our hearts, it sets off a chain reaction of compassion toward others.

The mystery of this antidote is that it is compulsively shared by those who have received it. In fact, the catalyst to ignite mercy's healing power is in the very act of giving it to others. We can certainly receive some healing power from mercy without letting it flow, but mercy that is horded is mercy that has not been truly experienced. Let's be like mirrors that receive mercy and immediately bless others with it.

My wife and I have been watching The Matthew Movie, which is a word-for-word account of the book of Matthew straight from the New International Version of the Bible. It is incredibly well produced and captures the spirit of Jesus as few movies have. While James was writing this section, he was reflecting upon the words of Jesus written in Matthew 18:21-35. Angela and I watched that part yesterday and my heart was greatly stirred by it. Jesus told a story to Peter concerning the Kingdom of Heaven that is incredibly difficult for me to swallow, but Jesus said it and we must do our best to take a hold of it.

"Then Peter came to him and asked, 'Lord, how often should I forgive someone who sins against me? Seven times?' 'No, not seven times,' Jesus replied, 'but seventy times seven! Therefore, the Kingdom of Heaven can be compared to a king who decided to bring his accounts up to date with servants who had borrowed money from him. In the process, one of his debtors was brought in who owed him millions of dollars. He couldn't pay, so his master ordered that he be sold—along with his wife, his children, and everything he owned—to pay the debt. But the man fell down before his master and begged him, "Please, be patient with me, and I will pay it all." Then his master was filled with pity for him, and he released him and forgave his debt. But when the man left the king, he went to a fellow servant who owed him a few thousand dollars. He grabbed him by the throat and demanded instant payment. His fellow servant fell down before him and begged for a little more time. "Be patient with me, and I will pay it," he pleaded. But his creditor wouldn't wait. He had the man arrested and put in prison until the debt could be paid in full. When some of the other servants saw this, they were distraught. They went to the king and told him everything that had happened. Then the king called in the man he had forgiven and said, "You evil servant! I forgave you that tremendous debt because you pleaded with me. Shouldn't you have mercy on your fellow servant, just as I had mercy on you?" Then the angry king sent the man to prison to be tortured until he had paid his entire debt'" (Matthew 18:21-34 NLT). Jesus abruptly ends the story with this thunderous proclamation: "That's what my heavenly Father will do to you if you refuse to forgive your brothers and sisters from your heart" (Matthew 18:35 NLT).

One of the most fascinating parts of this story is the comparison of debts. The first debtor, who represents all of us, is inexplicably excused from having to pay the equivalent of millions of dollars today. He then turns around and, in a mind-boggling reaction to forgiveness, demands the few thousand dollars from a servant who owed him. While this may seem ludicrous, I would contend that this is a regular occurrence in most of our lives . We celebrate our salvation in Christ and yet we decide to harbor grudges, jealousy and strife in our souls against others. No matter how evil we think someone's actions were toward us, isn't God still excusing us from having to pay a larger debt than the evil done against us? When we see the value of the mercy shown us in our lives, the entirety of the pain and hurt that we have experienced in our lives can begin to fade into the vastness of the forgiveness we have received.

If you don't feel that you have been able to harness the power of mercy in your life, I hope that Jesus' words provide you sufficient motivation to direct your heart towards his mercy. If you feel that you have a difficult time showing mercy to others, try to find areas where you have clogged the flow of God's mercy into your own life. Mercy is not earned. Allow it to flow freely into your heart, grasping tightly to the truth that is available for you.

Reflection, Prayer and Action

- **Reflection**: Are there certain sins you see as less than others? Take some time to meditate on the truth that every sin breaks the unity of the law.
- **Prayer**: "God, help me to recognize the sins in my life that I have been downplaying. Let me be aware of them and horrified by them. Then, because of your infinite mercy, I can ask for you to forgive me and you will! Also, make me the kind of person who, upon receiving this mercy, is quick to give mercy to others."
- **Action**: Pray for forgiveness for any sins you've committed and haven't asked for forgiveness for. Then, ask God to help you extend mercy to those who have hurt you or those you love.

James 2:14-26
Living by Faith through Works

"What good is it, my brothers, if someone says he has faith but does not have works? Can that faith save him? If a brother or sister is poorly clothed and lacking in daily food, and one of you says to them, 'Go in peace, be warmed and filled,' without giving them the things needed for the body, what good is that? So also faith by itself, if it does not have works, is dead. But someone will say, 'You have faith and I have works.' Show me your faith apart from your works, and I will show you my faith by my works. You believe that God is one; you do well. Even the demons believe—and shudder! Do you want to be shown, you foolish person, that faith apart from works is useless? Was not Abraham our father justified by works when he offered up his son Isaac on the altar? You see that faith was active along with his works, and faith was completed by his works; and the Scripture was fulfilled that says, 'Abraham believed God, and it was counted to him as righteousness'—and he was called a friend of God. You see that a person is justified by works and not by faith alone. And in the same way was not also Rahab the prostitute justified by works when she received the messengers and sent them out by another way? For as the body apart from the spirit is dead, so also faith apart from works is dead."
– James 2:14-26

"He will render to each one according to his works: to those who by patience in well-doing seek for glory and honor and immortality, he will give eternal life; but for those who are self-seeking and do not obey the truth, but obey unrighteousness, there will be wrath and fury."
– Romans 2:6-8

Tread Carefully

This particular section of James' letter has sparked much debate in the Christian community. It pivots around two questions that will initially create turmoil in our hearts if we examine them closely: "What good is it, my brothers, if someone says he has faith but does not have works? Can that faith save him?" (James 2:14). James' answer to both questions is "…faith apart from works is dead" (v. 26). On the surface, that answer may seem to contradict many truths of the Bible declares. It has even been said that the words that James wrote here actually destroy the message of the gospel. This section has been a lightning rod for ideas and controversies ever since it was written. It has even been the center of many discussions about apparent contradictions with scripture, especially in relation to those scriptures written by Paul. Just about every week I heard or read a verse that resonated with this topic and I eventually found that my Evernote account (where I catalogue all of my writing ideas) was flooded with content for this topic far beyond the other topics of the letter. Upon reflection, this doesn't surprise me. In fact, I shouldn't have expected anything less. I personally see this section as the central theme of the Christian life and of James' letter primarily because it so intimately reflects the heart, words and actions of Jesus.

As we walked through this extraordinary section, scrutinize each word that James wrote. Take the words of Jesus and biblical authors, such as Paul and Peter, and begin to project them all together onto the wall of your mind. What you will find is an exquisite pattern of thoughts that fortify, rather than weaken, James' discussion of works and faith. The message at the heart of this section is completely Christian. Some have twisted these words in order to draw people away from the glorious gospel and enslave them. Evil hands have often tried to morph these words into shackles of good deeds apart from justification in Christ. Stay alert and ask the Holy Spirit to guide you through this precarious but critical passage of James' letter.

Displaying Active Compassion towards Everyone

James' first example of faith and works continues in the same vein as his earlier talk on partiality and mercy but adds an element of positive action. Previously he focused on not disparaging and putting down those who are in need as well as extending mercy to those who sin against us. Now, in the example he gives of a fellow Christian being in need, his focus has shifted toward displaying our faith through active compassion. His concern is with those who speak loftily and bless others through their empty words and gestures but do not go out of their way to help as Jesus did. We are not called to simply be acquainted with the words of the law. Rather, we must galvanize the intent of the law in our own lives and prevail over the human tendency to just check the box. That is not what justifies us. Active compassion does not stop at merely undoing evil but seeks to make things better and holier. This compassion does not stop when things are just ok; it keeps going until everything is whole and complete and doesn't lack anything.

As with many virtues, the best way to start applying and demonstrating compassion is to practice it on the nearest Christians. As a matter of fact, Jesus declared that our loving and caring actions for other believers would be the defining, telltale characteristic of every follower of Christ: "A new commandment I give to you, that you love one another: just as I have loved you, you also are to love one another. By this all people will know that you are my disciples, if you have love for one another" (John 13:34). In other words, if we start our journey towards righteousness by internalizing and sharing God's love with Christians, we will begin to shine out in the darkness. No matter how small our acts of compassion and faith may seem, they are like a lighthouse in a dark bay. "You are the light of the world. A city set on a hill cannot be hidden. Nor do people light a lamp and put it under a basket, but on a stand, and it gives light to all in the house. In the same way, let your light shine before others, so that they may see your good works and give glory to your Father who is in heaven" (Matthew 5:14-16). To put it another way, compassion and good deeds spring out of love and give us the aroma of heaven with which others will identify us. The full effect of your efforts may never be obvious to you, but eternity will ring out with joy over every kind action you make towards other Christians. The mere act of saying, "Bless you" or "I'm praying for you" to another is vanity if it is not backed up by an army of positive exertions that fulfill the commandments of God to care for one another. "This is the love of God, that we keep his commandments. And his commandments are not burdensome. For everyone who has been born of God overcomes the world. And this is the victory that has overcome the world — our faith" (1 John 5:3–4). The eighteenth-century pastor and theologian Jonathan Edwards wrestled with this text and concluded, "Saving faith implies . . . love. . . . Our love to God enables us to overcome the difficulties that attend keeping God's commands — which shows that love is the main thing in saving faith, the life and power of it, by which it produces great effects."

Like ripples in a pond, your actions toward fellow believers will reverberate out into the lives of those around you who have not yet accepted Christ. However, while showing love to other Christians is a beautiful start, we must not run a quarter mile, stop, and say we ran a marathon. This next part is much harder. We are ultimately directed by Jesus to display his compassion to everyone. This is always essential and often painful. It is always easier to help others who are nice to us or share the same beliefs as us, but Jesus was aware of this and addressed it directly for us: "You have heard that it was said, 'You shall love your neighbor and hate your enemy.' But I say to you, Love your enemies and pray for those who persecute you, so that you may be sons of your Father who is in heaven. For he makes his sun rise on the evil and on the good, and sends rain on the just and on the unjust. For if you love those who love you, what reward do you have? Do not even the tax collectors do the same? And if you greet only your brothers, what more are you doing than others? Do not even the Gentiles do the same? You therefore must be perfect, as your heavenly Father is perfect" (Matthew 5:43-47). A few verses later, Jesus makes another bold statement: "But when you give to the needy, do not let your left hand know what your right hand is doing, so that your giving may be in secret. And your Father who sees in secret will reward you" (Matthew 6:3-4). Rather than saying, "If you give to the needy…", he declares, "But when you give to the needy…". In the middle of a statement about how to give, he enforces the duty and honor that we have to always give to those who are in need.

As a sort of footnote to this, I thought it would be fitting to share the most effective ways that I know to give to the needy. The most obvious way of giving to the needy is through money. While it is not inherently wrong to give money to people who are asking for it, you should be led by the Holy Spirit - and not just your emotions - to do give. The money you give may actually be used for what they're asking for, or it may end up enabling an addiction or other harmful activity. Instead of giving money, I would recommend taking the person out to lunch, giving them a hand with something, or helping them get somewhere. Although this method of giving is great, I would not recommend making it the only way that you give to the needy because it is probably not a consistent enough opportunity for you. Ideally, a majority of your giving would be done on a regular basis, either through money or your time. The most universally available method is to give monthly donations, in wisdom and discernment, to your local church and charities that you have researched and trust. Usually we are not the most well equipped or trained to help those in deepest need. Giving to organizations that specialize in areas like caring for the homeless, rescuing those who have been sexually abused, and building homes for widows or single mothers, can be the most effective way to help. And don't forget that you can volunteer to help those organizations! Whatever resource you have to give, give it all through faith in God and his glorious purpose, knowing that your faith will be greatly rewarded.

As with many virtues, there is more to the story than what we may initially think. Christian compassion isn't limited to "nice" or "good" deeds towards those who are less fortunate. The words of compassion, kindness, friendliness and acceptance have been shoved interchangeably into various situations until they have lost much of their meaning. Jesus' compassion, the compassion we should always strive to show, was not one of mere acceptance or kindness. Sometimes, his compassion looked downright mean on the surface. His compassion was not "nice" when he called the Pharisees a "brood of vipers" and his compassion was not "accepting" when he made a whip and drove all of the salespeople out of his father's house (Matthew 21:12-13, 23:33). The compassion that Jesus showed was not to pander to or condone evil, but to boldly alert people to the impending doom that they were marching into. His words were transformed into a blazing warning, shining out with righteous indignation and compassion that were his only option to get through to those who were just listening for a way to destroy Jesus. In this same spirit, James' genuine compassion shines brightly in chapter 5:1-6 as he throws a bucket of cold water on the slumbering, greedy people and implores them to leave their impatient ways (We'll get to that part near the end of this book).

What Comes First: Belief or Actions?

As we have seen through James' example of helping others, right believing leads to right actions. Good deeds are not enough on their own and right believing does not remain alive without right actions. To believe and not act on your belief would be like trying to create the color green without the color blue. Both faith and works are needed; they are not mutually exclusive in a Christian's life. If there are no works, there is no saving faith.

While it was necessary to say, that the last statement I made may have been misleading. Neither James nor I intend to taint the glorious gospel of substitution by inferring that our salvation comes from our works. The paradox is mentally suffocating at first: We cannot do anything to earn salvation and yet if we do not do anything it is evidence that we are not saved. How can James say this and not disintegrate the very truth of salvation!

We see in other parts of scripture that our works are not the determining factor in our salvation:

> "For by grace you have been saved through faith. And this is not your own doing; it is the gift of God, not a result of works, so that no one may boast. For we are his workmanship, created in Christ Jesus for good works, which God prepared beforehand, that we should walk in them" (Ephesians 2:8-10).

In his preaching, Jesus founded salvation squarely on belief in him, even starting out this particular thought with the potent "Truly, truly, I say to you…" statement, meaning that this information was vital to those who were listening:

"Truly, truly, I say to you, whoever hears my word and believes him who sent me has eternal life. He does not come into judgment, but has passed from death to life" (John 5:24).

This is difficult, but to help provide some clarity, I'd like to present the harmony between faith and works in the following way: Have you ever gone camping? While I am not particularly fond of camping, I have gone camping a few times and have enjoyed parts of it. One of the more memorable experiences I recall was a biking trip. My father, brother Marshall and I spent almost the entire day on our mountain bikes "bonsai-ing" through all kinds of ridiculous terrain in northern New Hampshire (I'm fairly certain that my dad coined the term "bonsai-ing"). The exhausting work was richly rewarded that night when we broke out the food that we had brought and started a glorious fire to cook the food on. We were covered with mud and chilling sweat, but we didn't mind so much. As long as the fire was burning that night, heat flowed out from it and it kept our conversations warm and our spirits high. The heat from the fire came from the flames and both occurred naturally together.

In the same way, James viewed faith and obedience as two effects of the same salvation. His view is bolstered by this statement in Gospel of John: "Whoever believes in the Son has eternal life; whoever does not obey the Son shall not see life, but the wrath of God remains on him." (John 3:36). You'll notice that John says "whoever believes" in the first sentence and then swaps "belief" with "obey" in the second sentence when he discusses what the opposite of belief looks like. In true Jewish style, John uses the pairing of two sentences to draw a direct inference between believing and action. Here is the point: When you have belief burning inside of your soul, you must act! You, like the fire, cannot help but exude enthusiasm and actions that reflect your belief.

However, works are not always the evidence of belief, just as heat doesn't necessarily mean that there is a fire. We should not be fooled into thinking that works are necessarily evidence of faith. After declaring that actions are essential to the Christian, James counters a false assumption that he sees coming: "But someone will say, 'You have faith and I have works.' Show me your faith apart from your works, and I will show you my faith by my works" (James 1:18). Nice actions are possible without faith, though they are useless in the eyes of God. However, when belief comes first, then good actions will start to be automatic and become holy before God.

Even Demons Believe

While belief in God is the cornerstone of our saving faith, James informs us in verse 19 that, "Even the demons believe – and shudder!" So there must be different levels and flavors of belief in God. While we as humans have been given revelation of God that puts us beyond excuse of ignorance (Romans 1:20), demons, having been angels before, had a much clearer view of who God is than we do, and yet they chose to reject him and follow the devil. Though we don't know exactly why, demons have decided to reject God and follow the devil. Instead of glorifying God and enjoying him forever, they have decided to become thieves, murderers and destroyers, just like the devil (John 10:10). Wouldn't a greater understanding of God have inspired all of the angels to remain serving God? Somehow, through events that are not explained in detail to us, these former angels saw God and opted to follow evil rather than good. My educated guess is that pride, the desire to be above everything else and to be our own God, darkened their hearts and motivated them to become traitors.

Whatever the situation, this ought to be a warning to us. I know that in my own soul there are thieving, hateful and destructive tendencies that when I give them full movement in my soul, I can see the appeal of evil. In those moments, I look at God as if I lived all my life in a cave and cannot stand to see the glorious, burning light emanating from his goodness. This is why I fear for those people who say, "If God would just talk to me, I would listen" or "I won't believe until I see him." If they continue to live in the darkness and do not cry out to God to prepare their hearts, their shriveled hearts may still reject God even when it would be impossible to deny his existence. "For everyone who does wicked things hates the light and does not come to the light, lest his works should be exposed. But whoever does what is true comes to the light, so that it may be clearly seen that his works have been carried out in God" (John 3:20-21). As it is, the demons have defected to a powerless leader and are franticly grasping at human souls in a futile attempt to overthrow God. The demons surely believe in God, but it is a terrifying reality for them. Not all types of belief lead to salvation any more than all types of roads lead to the same destination.

There are also those who express knowledge and understanding of God but do not back up their words with actions. This is known as "gnosis" or "head knowledge." In verse 14, James' expression is, "...if someone says he has faith..." not "...if someone has faith..." The key difference here is that it is possible to express, and even feel, a belief in Jesus as God without actually having that saving faith. This of course raises a red flag in my heart and my mind exclaims, "Then am I actually saved?" I am not saying that we should all be concerned on a daily basis with whether or not we are actually saved. Nevertheless, Jesus declared to us that we should expect our emotions, thoughts and actions to be steadily changed as we invite him into our heart more intimately. "And we all, with unveiled face, beholding the glory of the Lord, are being transformed into the same image from one degree of glory to another. For this comes from the Lord who is the Spirit" (2 Corinthians 3:18). If we only express faith with our mouths but do not see a steady, sometimes slow, transformation in our hearts to being like Jesus, I would say that we should seriously seek Jesus about whether or not we are actually walking in saving faith. In this excerpt from Pilgrim's Progress, the protagonist, Christian, is warning the character Faith about Talk, expresses a devotion to Christ but who is really just full of hot air and no action:

> This man is for any company, and for any talk; as he talketh now with you, so will he talk when he is on the ale-bench; and the more drink he hath in his crown, the more of these things he hath in his mouth; religion hath no place in his heart, or house, or conversation; all he hath lieth in his tongue, and his religion is, to make a noise therewith...remember the proverb, "They say and do not" (Matthew 23:3). But the kingdom of God is not in word, but in Power (1 Corinthians 4:20). He talketh of prayer, of

repentance, of faith, and of the new birth; but he knows but only to talk of them…For my part, I am of opinion, that he has, by his wicked life, caused many to stumble and fall; and will be, if God prevent not, the ruin of many more.

As I write this section, I feel the responsibility to not mislead you in one of two ways. I do not want you to spend your life in fear that your salvation is false. I also shutter to think that you would be oblivious to the dangerous situation you are in if you express faith in Jesus but do not cling to it. Thankfully, God has a beautiful solution to this dilemma: Seek the Holy Spirit. "In him you also, when you heard the word of truth, the gospel of your salvation, and believed in him, were sealed with the promised Holy Spirit, who is the guarantee of our inheritance until we acquire possession of it, to the praise of his glory" (Ephesians 1:13-14). It is through the Holy Spirit that we can be assured of our salvation with absolute certainty. If you have read this section and have become convicted of having false faith, do not despair! The Holy Spirit has brought you under that conviction in order that you may be set free through genuine saving faith. All you have to do is ask.

Becoming a Superstar

Because our godly actions are evidence of our saving faith, we can potentially become concerned about our salvation because we continue to sin and can't seem to consistently act like Jesus. This concern may lead us to believe that we do not have saving faith and then become consumed and obsessed with performing good actions to prove our faith. Of course, each of us must initially wrestle with whether or not we have truly accepted Jesus as Lord of our lives. Once we make that decision to enter the Kingdom of Heaven, we are at a point where we simultaneously have saving faith and are yet still tethered down by our old habits, thoughts, and stubborn neural pathways. How are we to prove that we have saving faith if we are still doing what we did when we did not have saving faith?

This is where the doctrine of sanctification comes in. Our justification before God is the instantaneous event wherein, by accepting Jesus as Lord, we have all of our sins removed and receive as a gift all of the righteousness of Jesus. This is not earned and it is not a drawn-out process; rather, it is a free gift. However, our sanctification is another story. Because we have received Jesus' righteousness that covers us like a blanket, God sees Jesus when he looks at us. That was a necessary starting point for us to be able to change to become like Jesus, but we all know that there is still much work to be done to allow God to change who we are beneath the blanket of grace. It is only through the covering of justification that our souls have the right environment to become sanctified, which means to have holiness inside of us.

Through Christ's saving grace, he is working a mighty change in the hearts of his beloved. While we start as only being righteous because of Jesus' work, we begin to have such a transformation in us that righteous deeds begin to trickle, and eventually gush forth. It is not God's ultimate plan to force righteous deeds upon us, but to give us the ability and inspiration to grow because of his unconditional love. It is the process of tending to the garden of our souls with Jesus' guidance to begin to see a bumper crop of holiness rise up in our lives. As we saw already in the beginning of James' letter, it is through the soil of his goodness and the endurance we gain from the fertilizer of trials and adversity that we see this happen. Christ desires to remind us when our steadfastness is fully developed, we will be perfect and complete, lacking in nothing (James 1:4). In the end, we will see these words from the book of Revelation fulfilled about each of us who follows Jesus: "'Hallelujah! For the Lord our God the Almighty reigns. Let us rejoice and exult and give him the glory, for the marriage of the Lamb has come, and his Bride has made herself ready; it was granted her to clothe herself with fine linen, bright and pure'— for the fine linen is the righteous deeds of the saints" (Revelation 19:6b-8).

As with many virtues, we are given an example to emulate. In the region of faith, Abraham is our resident superstar. He started off modestly enough by obeying one commandment: "Go from your country and your kindred and your father's house to the land that I will show you" (Genesis 12:1). Everything after that, even his mistakes and shortcomings, was part of a process that made him into a man of faith. His faith was cultivated in the rich soil of obedience. He was not automatically full of faith but steadily embraced it through glorifying God and trusting in his promises. He became convinced of God's good intentions toward him and intentionally stuck with his faith through seasons that lacked evidence of God's faithfulness. He resolved to embrace the promises of God, held to them with gusto, and became the superstar of faith one step at a time. "No unbelief made [Abraham] waver concerning the promise of God, but he grew strong in his faith as he gave glory to God, fully convinced that God was able to do what he had promised. That is why his faith was 'counted to him as righteousness.' But the words 'it was counted to him' were not written for his sake alone, but for ours also. It will be counted to us who believe in him who raised from the dead Jesus our Lord, who was delivered up for our trespasses and raised for our justification" (Romans 4:20-25). Paul again highlights Abraham's faith: "Does he who supplies the Spirit to you and works miracles among you do so by works of the law, or by hearing with faith—just as Abraham 'believed God, and it was counted to him as righteousness?'" (Galatians 3:5-6).

Guided by the Holy Spirit, James did not only mention Abraham in his discussion of faith. He calls upon someone who you would not think would make the cut in a celebration of faith: A prostitute from the fallen city of Jericho named Rahab. When Israel was finally ready to enter into the home that God promised them, Canaan, messengers were sent into Jericho to spy it out. While they were nearly discovered, it was Rahab who hid them and redirected their enemies to protect them, and then let them escape. God created a seed of faith inside of Rahab that began to germinate when she acted upon it. This unassuming act of faith earned her an honorable mention in the most important book ever written. I'm sure that she had no idea that her act of faith would have that sort of effect. What this says to me is that our faith, being a force that joins with the power of God, cannot be overestimated in its impact. You may never receive praise for your faith, but you are shaping eternity through it.

Rehab was included here so that we don't assume that achieving this kind of faith is either too difficult or for the "spiritually elite." By putting the faith of Rahab on display, he topples any rationalization we may put up that says that we cannot or should not or will not encounter and embrace saving faith. Each of us has the opportunity to set out on a journey of immense faith and action no matter where our starting point is.

Reflection, Prayer and Action

- **Reflection**: Have you been trying to get God's favor by doing good things? Are you doing good actions inspired by your faith, or are you doing them in hopes of getting something from God? Alternatively, have you been saying that you have faith but your life doesn't show any of the resulting actions?
- **Prayer**: "God, help me to embrace the union of faith and works in my life. I desire to believe in you wholeheartedly and, from that place of excitement and gratitude, do amazing things in your name."
- **Action**: Ask the Holy Spirit to give you guidance on what step of faith you need to take next. You may already know what it is. In that case, act on it. If your life hasn't been producing good actions, seek first to press into God and pray for your faith to be ignited. Then go out and do something with thankfulness for your salvation at the forefront of your mind.

James Chapter 3

This middle chapter targets two critical topics: The power of words and the need for godly wisdom. These two themes reach into many areas of our lives and have tremendous impact, so James takes his time to unpack them. Our souls are in great need of this instruction and James has prepared a feast that, if enjoyed fully, will nourish and assist us for our entire lives.

James 3:1-12
Taming the Tongue

"Not many of you should become teachers, my brothers, for you know that we who teach will be judged with greater strictness. For we all stumble in many ways. And if anyone does not stumble in what he says, he is a perfect man, able also to bridle his whole body. If we put bits into the mouths of horses so that they obey us, we guide their whole bodies as well. Look at the ships also: though they are so large and are driven by strong winds, they are guided by a very small rudder wherever the will of the pilot directs. So also the tongue is a small member, yet it boasts of great things. How great a forest is set ablaze by such a small fire! And the tongue is a fire, a world of unrighteousness. The tongue is set among our members, staining the whole body, setting on fire the entire course of life, and set on fire by hell. For every kind of beast and bird, of reptile and sea creature, can be tamed and has been tamed by mankind, but no human being can tame the tongue. It is a restless evil, full of deadly poison. With it we bless our Lord and Father, and with it we curse people who are made in the likeness of God. From the same mouth come blessing and cursing. My brothers, these things ought not to be so. Does a spring pour forth from the same opening both fresh and salt water? Can a fig tree, my brothers, bear olives, or a grapevine produce figs? Neither can a salt pond yield fresh water."
– James 3:1-12

"Set a guard, O Lord, over my mouth; keep watch over the door of my lips! Do not let my heart incline to any evil, to busy myself with wicked deeds in company with men who work iniquity, and let me not eat of their delicacies!"
– Psalm 141:3-4

"Words are, of course, the most powerful drug used by mankind."
– Rudyard Kipling

Word Play

Anne Sullivan may not be a familiar name to you, but her legacy as a teacher probably is. Born in 1866, she received her education at the Perkins School for the Blind and soon became the instructor for a girl who had become both deaf and blind before her second birthday. The doctors had determined that it was either scarlet fever or meningitis that caused this incredible loss. Anne was put to the test every day by her student's outbursts and general lack of interest in Anne's attempts to teach her. While the girl had created her own rudimentary signs for communicating with people, her ability to communicate was severely limited. She didn't realize that Anne was trying to open up the world to her. One day, Anne put the girl's hand under a spout, pumped some water onto her hand, and then formed the sign language symbol for "water" in the girl's hand. This may initially have seemed to Anne like just another disappointing failure waiting to happen, but that was the moment where everything changed. It was as if the water had finally broken through into the girl's consciousness and brought with it the light of knowledge. The girl finally realized what Anne had been doing all along. That entire day, the girl ran around grasping everything she could find and wordlessly pleading for Anne to show her what sign to use for it. Anne's student, Helen Keller, went on to become a prolific author, philosopher, celebrity and Christian, all because of Anne's perseverance and careful instruction.

Imagine where we would be without teachers like Anne Sullivan? Teachers like her have provided instruction, good examples, strength and encouragement to every type of student. Indeed, this is a wonderful thing: the world needs more teachers like Anne Sullivan. However, we know that there are no perfect teachers, and since they too are held to the standard of their words, we are presented with a dilemma when it comes to broken humanity. As James says, "For we all stumble in many ways" (James 3:2). Teachers face many obstacles, with the most noticeable ones being pride and laziness.

Humans are prone to speak from hearts of pride rather than of love. The teacher-student relationship places the teacher and student in positions of sharing and receiving, with the teacher having the greatest responsibility. Through the corruption of sin, the position of teacher has often been turned into a way to hold knowledge as a scepter, ruling over others with it. The proud teacher desires to know more and to be better than others for no other reason than to be above others, and so novelty gets exalted above truth and accuracy, arrogance above humility, and fanaticism above substance. This kind of teacher would rather acquire gifts in pride than receive them humbly from the ultimate source, as Simon the Enchanter attempted to do:

> Now when Simon saw that the Spirit was given through the laying on of the apostles' hands, he offered them money, saying, "Give me this power also, so that anyone on whom I lay my hands may receive the Holy Spirit." But Peter said to him, "May your silver perish with you, because you thought you could obtain the gift of God with money!" (Acts 8:18-20).

Rather than seeking to understand how the Holy Spirit was given, Simon saw it as an opportunity to become an even more powerful enchanter. He desired to skip the process that the disciples went through to receive the Holy Spirit and jump straight to "wielding the power". He was deceived in his comprehension of the Holy Spirit and his soul flashed its true, self-consumed colors at the sight of God's power. Victor Frankl, a renowned Jewish neurologist and psychiatrist as well as a Holocaust survivor, saw this same danger in the teachers of his day:

> I am absolutely convinced that the gas chambers of Auschwitz, Treblinka, and Maidanek were ultimately prepared not in some ministry or other in Berlin, but rather at the desks and in the lecture halls of nihilistic scientists and philosophers. ("Victor Frankl at Ninety: An Interview," in First Things, April 1995, p. 41.)

Ideas and words have consequences – for good or bad – and it is the responsibility of a teacher to be careful not to let ego and fascination create something hideous and damaging. Words have formidable power.

While pride is one serious hurdle for the teacher, laziness is another. Teaching quite often takes a substantial amount of preparation time and, if skipped or glossed over, can lead to providing misinformation, incomplete thoughts, and skewed perspectives that may damage an audience.

The words that teachers have spoken have shaped my life over the years. Think back on those in authority over you who have said things that greatly shaped your life. Are there moments burned into your neural pathways that are incredibly emotional? I hope you have many good memories about past teachers, but I know that's not always the case. I've heard many stories about teachers declaring in front of the class that a particular student was dumb. Those words, whether spoken aloud or written in a report card, had significant potential to hurt, and they often did. When I think about it, I wonder what was going through the teacher's mind at that moment. I contemplate how many of those teachers intended for their words to have such consequences. Were they genuinely intending to scar that student? Were they just distracted, upset by something else, or just plain tired? Of course, any reasoning for saying the hurtful words does not change the effect it had upon the student, but if it was unintentional it shows that carelessness can cause just as much harm as pride in many cases. Students are ultimately responsible for how they respond to the criticism, but that does not mean that the teachers are not responsible for cutting deep wounds with their words.

John Stuart Mill, an English philosopher, wrote, "Both teachers and learners go to sleep at their post as soon as there is no enemy in the field." In other words, it doesn't take much for us to be lulled into a place of complacency. As soon as we're not challenged or we get tired, mental and emotional slumber are about to come knocking. After all, constant vigilance in any occupation or activity is exhausting and unsustainable. Teachers cannot be expected to naturally sustain perfection in such an arduous activity as teaching.

Through various events and accounts in the New Testament, we find that the Pharisees and religious leaders of Jesus' day were both prideful and careless in their teaching. Jesus, having seen the hypocrisy and damaging effects of their words, spoke this against them: "Either make the tree good and its fruit good, or make the tree bad and its fruit bad, for the tree is known by its fruit. You brood of vipers! How can you speak good, when you are evil? For out of the abundance of the heart the mouth speaks. The good person out of his good treasure brings forth good, and the evil person out of his evil treasure brings forth evil. I tell you, on the day of judgment people will give account for every careless word they speak, for by your words you will be justified, and by your words you will be condemned" (Matthew 12:33-37).

Before we move onto the main point that James is making in this section, I'd like to make it clear that I have no grudges or qualms with the teaching community. I greatly admire those who have invested their lives in the betterment of others. I say all of these things to point out the impossibility of perfection for any teacher, whether they fall because of pride, laziness or some other stumbling block. The point is that all teachers will mess up at one point or another whether they realize it or not.

If you don't fill out forms with "Teacher" as your occupation, you may feel that this particular bit isn't applicable to you. If you feel that way, I would ask you this: Have you ever given advice to someone about his or her life, marriage, relationship, job, kids, etc.? If you have, I would say that in that moment, you became a teacher. James is challenging us all as teachers in one capacity or another. Obviously, there are those in the school systems, churches, work, and other places that teach more often than others, but not having the title of "teacher" or "pastor" does not mean that your words are exempt from this instruction. After all, James includes all of us when he says, "For we all stumble in many ways. And if anyone does not stumble in what he says, he is a perfect man, able also to bridle his whole body" (James 3:2).

In the end, anyone who gives instruction, guidance or advice to someone else clearly has the devil crouching at their door, waiting to trap them in pride, negligence perhaps or some other sin. By placing this topic directly after the discussion of faith and works, it appears that Jesus showed James the tie-in between faith, works and words. Actions are often louder than words, but as we'll see in this section, our words not only shape others' lives, but also determine our own lives' directions and impacts.

In my own experience, the ratio of my thoughts to the actions I take is pretty high. There is much more going on in my mind and emotions at any given time than what I show through my actions. Jesus illustrated this through a metaphor: "The good person out of the good treasure of his heart produces good, and the evil person out of his evil treasure produces evil, for out of the abundance of the heart his mouth speaks" (Luke 6:45). Notice that Bible verse doesn't say, "The mouth speaks exactly what the heart is thinking" but rather "out of the abundance of the heart", meaning that it is what we fill ourselves with and meditate on that begins to leak and then pour out of us. We may see others or ourselves as being "good" because the actions are "clean", but often there is evil brewing in us that has not yet reached a tipping point. This verse is pinpointing the problem that we have: We assume that something cannot exist because we cannot see it or completely understand it. My challenge to you is to examine the condition of your heart and find where evil may be starting to bubble up. You probably won't have to look hard at all.

So we see that our words are an overflow of our thoughts and emotions, but that is only part of the story. Our thoughts do construct our words, but our words also shape our thoughts and lives. James presents two examples at the beginning of the chapter to illustrate the powerful directive force of the tongue. In both examples of the horse's bridle and the ship's rudder, he identifies the physical smallness of the item and therefore the perceived insignificance of the power that they each have. Then, he reminds us how these two items, though physically small, contain the potential to direct the energy of both the horse and the ship; they are the guiding force. The horse is propelled by powerful legs and the ship by gusts of wind, but the bridle and the rudder are what channel power. In the same way, our hearts are full of potential energy that is waiting to be released. The existence of that energy is important, but if it is never unleashed or if it is misappropriated, the power inside of us is wasted. Our tongues shape our lives and direct our paths.

It may seem strange to you – it still seems strange to me – that our tongues would have such power. Why doesn't James focus on our thoughts and intentions rather than our tongues? Aren't our hearts and minds the driving forces behind all of our actions and words? This is certainly true, but God has divinely ordained that the firing of synapses and the physical movement of jaw muscle, tongue and vocal cord have the same sort of power that God's words have. After all, we were created in his image. The words of God – not merely his thoughts and emotions – were what brought the world into existence and formed vegetation, animals, humans and everything else that we see and cannot see (Genesis 1-2). It was the word of God that directed the path of Abraham and his descendants to their destiny through his spoken promises. It was the Word of God that put on skin, bone and muscle and lived among humanity in the person of Jesus.

So which is more important: Faith, actions or words? As we discovered in chapter two, merely saying we are saved doesn't make us saved, so we know that words by themselves are not able to accomplish everything. However, we also learned that good intentions and thoughts do not accomplish anything on their own either. It is through the marriage of our will and our words that the power of both is unleashed. Like in the example of the horse, we must start moving in order to make our words effective, but if we simply go off in any direction with our words and intentions contradicting each other, we will fall flat. Likewise, if we speak many words without meaning them, we get nowhere and are just flailing around in one spot, yanking our bridle back and forth with no progress. We are far too casual with our words and desperately unaware of their power.

So how does this marriage between faith, actions and words work? Our words can harness our lives effectively in a few ways. We can speak truth over ourselves when we are not entirely convinced of it, reminding ourselves of what we know is true. If we truly believe in Christ, there will still be times that we doubt or are pulled away from active faith. In those times, we must redirect our energy back toward Jesus by declaring scriptures about Jesus' divinity, compassion, faithfulness and love to ourselves. I often find myself worn out and feeling as though I have been walking by myself, with Jesus nowhere to be found. In those moments, the thing that helps me the most is declaring Jesus' presence with me and the fortifying strength that he desires to give me if only I accept it.

Another way our words can have great impact is through intercessory prayer, which means that our words are directed toward God asking him to change something for his glory, whether it be to heal someone, improve a financial situation, or have someone meet Jesus. Rather than just "wishing" something into existence, which is useless, our verbal petitions to God are potent and will be responded to.

The Fiery Wheel of Life

We've gone over a few examples of how to harness the power of our tongues, but if you have been alive for any length of time, you know that it is quite challenging to be consistent in controlling our tongues. In the Douay–Rheims Bible, James 3:6 reads: "And the tongue is a fire, a world of iniquity. The tongue is placed among our members, which defileth the whole body, and inflameth the wheel of our nativity, being set on fire by hell." Whether your version says "wheel of nativity" or "course of life", the idea is the same: Our words can encompass and permeate our entire lives with sin and danger. We're not talking about something that has a limited scope; its effects inundate every bit of our existence.

What we say is incredibly important and can shape our lives in ways we may never understand fully. The term "wheel of nativity" is a potent image that has helped me understand the interconnectedness of my life.

I'm a fan of many types of movies, including good Westerns. If Clint Eastwood shows up slinging a six-shooter and talking out of the side of his mouth, that's even better. If you've watched any movies that were based in that era or earlier, you've probably seen those rickety wagons rolling along with wooden wheels. All of those wheels had the same basic concept: an outer rim, spokes, and a hub.

A wheel's rim is literally where the rubber meets the road. It provides the traction to keep the load stable and it also overcomes the problem of friction by rotating rather than being dragged. Instead of forcing the horse to pull the load along the ground, the wheels transfer the energy forward over many types of terrain.

The next essential component of a wheel is the spoke. While one wheel may have six spokes and another may have a few dozen, the principle of the spokes stays the same. Its job is to connect the rim to the hub, and the spokes' rigidity and organization determine the shape that the wheel takes. If manufactured correctly, all of them will be identical and maintain integrity under stress caused by the vehicle's weight. If manufactured incorrectly – or damaged and not repaired – the weight of the load will be distributed more to certain spokes than others, which will cause strained spokes to bend or snap. This will lead to a warped or broken rim, which would make the wagon incredibly hard to steer (especially if the wheel has become a collection of broken parts).

The last part of the wheel is the hub. This is where the energy is transferred from the load and distributed to the spokes. If this part is broken or warped, a few things could happen: 1) The wheel could just fall off of the axle and ground the wagon, 2) the load will likely overload some of the spokes, making them snap and bend, or 3) the entire wheel would rotate so unevenly that the cart would be un-steerable.

The workings of a wheel can be used as a metaphor for the workings of our lives. Firstly, I would like you to imagine the hub is your heart. This is where you are connected to God when you are in right relationship with him. If your heart is not connected firmly to God, it will eventually become a useless, immobile piece of hardware.

Secondly, see the spokes as your thoughts. This is how your thoughts are distributed to your life. If you have only one obsession in your life and you leave behind all of the important Christian disciplines, you will be like a wheel with only one spoke and will soon fall apart. Your mind is inundated with thoughts of all kinds. If you do not fight, your life will become unwieldy and heavy with clutter and distraction.

Lastly, imagine the rim as your actions and words. The energy from your heart gets transferred to your thoughts and subsequently thrust outward into your words and actions, where they are visible to the world. The rules of human nature – which are similar to physics in many ways – dictate that energy from your heart is eventually transferred into the things you do and say. Therefore, I find it odd that people would lie to themselves and say that their private thoughts do not have any effect on anyone. When I let my heart slip away from a perfect union with God, my entire being gets out of whack and I am left wobbling, dissatisfied and frustrated. If our hearts aren't solidly connected to God, everything in our lives becomes inflamed. When I keep a particular thought as a primary focus, I know – whether for good or bad – it will begin to impact the shape of my actions and words. If I speak unconstructively from the abundance of my heart, I should not expect to have a life free from hurt.

This does not mean that bad things only happen to us when we invite evil into our vocabulary, but to leave this out of the equation would be foolish. Only when we add up all these different factors do we come up with the proper sum. God designed our tongues as creators, but that does not mean we cannot use it to create hurtful situations, chaos, or deadly situations for family members and friends. We are playing with matches that will either create a bonfire to warm us or a forest fire that will devour us.

The Fresh Spring

On September 27, 1962, Rachel Carson published a book that would drastically change the future landscape of chemical use in agriculture. The book was called Silent Spring and detailed the devastating effects of a pesticide called dichlorodiphenyltrichloroethane, or DDT, upon wildlife, which was especially true for birds. While DDT was effective at killing mosquitos and other harmful bugs, it also slowly poisoned most animals that were exposed to it either by swimming in it or by eating bugs that were exposed to it. Birds began dying off at alarming rates in areas where DDT was sprayed and the US Government was not reacting to the warnings of reports that showed this. Rachel wrote Silent Spring primarily to awaken the public and inspire outcry that would result in the elimination of this harmful chemical's use.

Up until the end of chapter 3 of James' letter, it appears as though the world is inevitably going to be burned down and destroyed by the ravenous, untamable nature of our words, However, the crux of this text is in the last few verses. While we have heard of the power of our words and have observed the potentially corrosive nature of the tongue, the solution seems to be out of reach. He says, "Does a spring pour forth from the same opening both fresh and salt water? Can a fig tree, my brothers, bear olives, or a grapevine produce figs? Neither can a salt pond yield fresh water" (James 3:11-12). This is a reiteration of Jesus' teaching: "Beware of false prophets, who come to you in sheep's clothing but inwardly are ravenous wolves. You will recognize them by their fruits. Are grapes gathered from thornbushes, or figs from thistles? So, every healthy tree bears good fruit, but the diseased tree bears bad fruit. A healthy tree cannot bear bad fruit, nor can a diseased tree bear good fruit. Every tree that does not bear good fruit is cut down and thrown into the fire. Thus you will recognize them by their fruits" (Matthew 7:15-20). If we are not careful, we may end up thinking that if we have become bad or tainted in any way, we no longer can produce the fruit of holy lives. This would certainly be true without God, but now that Jesus is dwelling in us, we have the opportunity to redeem the poisoned spring and start producing life again.

First and most significantly, the cleanup project involves transferring your source to God. Instead of relying on the spring of your soul, have your water shipped in from the unending, ever ready and waiting fountain of God's mercy. Our souls need his fresh, crystal clear water to thrive, so why would we go on mucking about in our own self-reliance? All of the other steps are founded on this concept.

Secondly, we must hold back from speaking what we don't understand or cannot activate in our own lives. We ought to internalize what we are going to share before we declare that others must follow it. This does not mean that we must be perfect before we can be of use to others. The dilemma that we run into is that we can easily sidestep our own process of sanctification by forcing guidance upon others in order to feel superior to them. Our natural tendency is to want to be better than others (this is called pride), but God has not called us to compare our holiness with others. We ought to speak into others' lives, but not to bloat our spirit with pride. Instead, the measuring stick that we must keep as our standard is the word of the Holy Spirit inside of us. We will not be judged according to our elevation in relation to others but rather according to extent that we allowed holiness to grow in our hearts through humility. Counteract pride and laziness in your life so that you can be ready to teach as the Holy Spirit guides you.

Finally, the process of sanctification is what brings about the ultimate goal of God's work in us: To make us pure and holy. This long-term goal of God's is audacious as it is beautiful. By making him our source and holding back from further polluting our souls, we can embrace the process of cleansing and renewing our minds.

He will not do it without our consent, but we can only do it with him. This continual process leads to the purifying of our souls and the appearance of holiness, to our great delight. As Job said, "Yet the righteous holds to his way, and he who has clean hands grows stronger and stronger" (Job 17:9).

Reflection, Prayer and Action

- **Reflection**: Do you feel in control of your tongue? Have you been intentional about sanctifying the words you say? Have you started to transfer your source of strength to God? Are you starting to see the display of holiness in what you say?
- **Prayer**: "God, I desire to use my words to praise you, to build others up, and to shape my life into the image of Jesus. I need your grace in order to remove the darkness in my soul. Help me to be a steward of your glory through what I say."
- **Action**: Pray each day this week for God to give you the desire and ability to make him your source. As you go about your day, take just a little bit longer before you say anything so that you can be sure you are going to say something that will benefit others. Finally, evaluate your heart to see where you may be unwilling to control your tongue. Pray over those areas of your heart and ask God to soften them to his divine purpose.

James 3:13-18
Galvanizing Your Life with Wisdom

"Who is wise and understanding among you? By his good conduct let him show his works in the meekness of wisdom. But if you have bitter jealousy and selfish ambition in your hearts, do not boast and be false to the truth. This is not the wisdom that comes down from above, but is earthly, unspiritual, demonic. For where jealousy and selfish ambition exist, there will be disorder and every vile practice. But the wisdom from above is first pure, then peaceable, gentle, open to reason, full of mercy and good fruits, impartial and sincere. And a harvest of righteousness is sown in peace by those who make peace."
– James 3:13-18

"Let no one deceive himself. If anyone among you thinks that he is wise in this age, let him become a fool that he may become wise. For the wisdom of this world is folly with God. For it is written, 'He catches the wise in their craftiness,' and again, 'The Lord knows the thoughts of the wise, that they are futile.' So let no one boast in men..."
– 1 Corinthians 3:18-21a

"Your words were found, and I ate them, and your words became to me a joy and the delight of my heart, for I am called by your name, O Lord, God of hosts."
– Jeremiah 15:16

Exhortation to Godly Wisdom

Whenever I shop for food, I try to get the most for my money as I can while still filling my shopping cart with healthy things. Most of my time is spent comparing the price per pound of one item to the next to maximize my money's value. Occasionally I've caught myself spending far too much time doing this, but I'm steadily finding a good balance. What does "price per pound" mean anyways? How can I be sure that I'm actually getting a pound? Who determines how much a pound weighs? Recently, I read an article on Wikipedia about how they keep the standard kilogram from changing. Somewhere on this planet, there is an airtight box that contains the universal standard kilogram. The conditions that it is in are designed to limit the amount of change occurring to the standard as much as possible. This is essential because if the standard changed even a little bit, there would be no way of ensuring that anything was weighed properly. In a perfect world, the standard would never change and could always be used to test if derivative standards were inaccurate.

In this section, James flings the doors open to a room that holds one of the most important universal standards: True wisdom. James brought us to the doorway to wisdom in James 1:5-8 and showed us how to knock. Now we get a chance to meet wisdom and discover the sharp juxtaposition of Godly wisdom and worldly wisdom. As James rips through the fog and grabs hold of the truth, you'll see that there is no ambiguity between the two.

In my mind, chapter 3 has been where the letter really picks up momentum. The various topics that have been shared over the last few chapters start to become intimately intertwined. This is where James weaves them together even more tightly. Here, we see him intertwining wisdom, works, impartiality and tongue taming into a glorious display of right living based on right believing. Verse 13 is an amalgamation of several challenges that Jesus has revealed to us thus far: "Who is wise and understanding among you? By his good conduct let him show his works in the meekness of wisdom" (James 3:13).

Dangerous "Wisdom"

God's true wisdom is absolute and has no rival. Many have tried to substitute their own cunning and cleverness for this wisdom. As we see in the Bible and in our own lives, that approach never ends well, in this life or in eternity. "For the foolishness of God is wiser than men, and the weakness of God is stronger than men" (1 Corinthians 1:25).

The life-giving river of Godly wisdom is flowing right through the center of humanity, but many people have tried creating artificial irrigation canals to try to separate the goodness of wisdom from its creator. They want the benefits of wisdom without having to be close to God. As humans, we desire to live well and yet live in sin. We read self-help books without also coming to God to heal us. We obsess over financial magazines without putting God first. We create new ways to have "safe sex" while keeping God's plan for marriage out of the picture. The resulting polluted take on wisdom has poisoned many hearts and distorted views of what a healthy life looks like. In the end, if we take God out of the picture, we are left with a wisdom that is "earthly, unspiritual, demonic" (James 3:15).

To put it another way, humanity has tried to genetically modify the truth to bring about a better harvest for ourselves. Countless hours are spent on finding ways to eliminate God from the soil of our hearts and grow spiritual sustenance on our own. It may appear to work for some people, but I know that each time I've done that, my soul eventually chokes on what I had intended to nourish me. We think that we can tear away bits of God's wisdom and superglue them onto our own desires and have something beautiful grow. Instead, we end up nurturing a spiritual chimera that will turn on us.

Is it possible that pursuing a godly life is difficult primarily because we have removed ourselves so far from the standard of truth that we don't know how much our own souls weigh? Is it possible that there is something unspiritual lurking within our daily habits because we have not fully accepted the wisdom from God? James promises that jealousy and self-centered motivations breed chaos and revolting sin.

In this way, people everywhere are gaining knowledge in order to improve their lives, but knowledge is not the same as wisdom. While they are certainly intertwined, they are far from being equal. Jesus dealt harshly with wisdom-less knowledge when he saw it in the Pharisees, who were the religious leaders of the time: "Woe to you, blind guides, who say, 'If anyone swears by the temple, it is nothing, but if anyone swears by the gold of the temple, he is bound by his oath.' You blind fools! For which is greater, the gold or the temple that has made the gold sacred? And you say, 'If anyone swears by the altar, it is nothing, but if anyone swears by the gift that is on the altar, he is bound by his oath.' You blind men! For which is greater, the gift or the altar that makes the gift sacred?" (Matthew 23:16-19).

The Pharisees had warped their perspective and completely missed the eminence of the temple over the gold in the temple. They had gotten so far into the intellectual weeds that they couldn't tell what was really important. Information and knowledge will never be as important as wisdom. Knowledge is like a collection of notes; wisdom is what tells us how to play them. Our lives will either end up being a symphony or a cacophony. The deciding factor will always be whether or not we are living from the wisdom that God gives us.

The Wisdom from Above

When James defines the "wisdom from above", he is stating that the wisdom we should desire to gain is from God and God alone. As we learned in the beginning of the letter, this wisdom just needs to be asked for and God will provide it to us. This wisdom will probably bring about drastic changes in your lifestyle, relationships, money management and most other choices. However, there is a distinction between wisdom and the good things that come from it. If you want to make a cup of coffee in a Keurig or other single-cup coffee system, you know that the cup needs to go into the intake and then hot water is run through the machine and into your mug. Imagine if you saw me place a Keurig cup into my mug and then pour hot water over it. You would probably walk over to me and say something like, "I don't think that's how it works…" You see, we need to follow the right instructions to get the system to work properly. In the same way, God has designed our souls and the system of wisdom to interact in a certain way. If we try to earn God's wisdom instead of simply asking for it, we will end up with a mess on our hands, or at the very least lost time and opportunities. If we try to strive after these things with human energy, we will end up disillusioned.

As we reflect on verse 13, we see a beam of hope for the self-centered soul. James appeals to our desire to be wise and understanding, then instructs us to do good things in meekness and wisdom. But what does this have to do with overcoming selfishness and jealousy? It not only relates to these topics, but is the killing blow to selfishness and jealousy. To bolster this thought, here are some of Paul's words in his second letter to the church in Corinth:

> And God is able to make all grace abound to you, so that having all sufficiency in all things at all times, you may abound in every good work. (2 Corinthians 9:8)

In other words, God is here all the time to inspire us to take hold of adventure and help us follow through. In James 3:13 we see a mention of wisdom being the catalyst behind good works and we learned in James 1:5 that wisdom originates in God. He gives us the power of wisdom. God is here and available to provide for all of our needs. He not only gives us wisdom for our benefit, but also that we may be a benefit to those around us. Initially, I find that to be counterintuitive, but this is where the gospel kicks in. God knows that we must receive from him to be happy, but he also knows that if we only receive from him without blessing others, we will become stagnant and substantially unhappy. Our souls were designed to be outlets, not cul-de-sacs. His sufficiency and grace are available all the time for this express purpose. He wants to make us happy, but not in the way we were trained in our culture. He wants us to experience the truth that stands triumphantly beside Jesus' words, "It is more blessed to give than to receive" (Acts 20:35).

When this truth gets absorbed by us, it becomes not only a comfort and a safe haven but also a weapon against the howling of our souls to invest in ourselves and leave nothing for others. "But as for you, O man of God, flee these things. Pursue righteousness, godliness, faith, love, steadfastness, gentleness. Fight the good fight of the faith. Take hold of the eternal life to which you were called and about which you made the good confession in the presence of many witnesses" (1 Timothy 6:11-12). The bitter jealousy and selfish ambition that are naturally ravenous in us are pale and shriveled in comparison to the cry of joy in our hearts when we give. This is because we can trust that God is right there with millions of boxes marked "Everything Your Soul Needs" just waiting for you to be empty so he can fill you. It is his joy to see you give your all to others because it gives him room to fill you again. "And let us not grow weary of doing good, for in due season we will reap, if we do not give up. So then, as we have opportunity, let us do good to everyone, and especially to those who are of the household of faith" (Galatians 6:9-10).

An additional factor that must be considered is that those with Godly wisdom are inherently meek. We see this in the second half of James 3:13: "By his good conduct let him show his works in the meekness of wisdom". When we truly see the world from God's perspective, we no longer desire to puff up certain things or put down others. With God's wisdom, things are what they are and there is no rivalry or confusion. Our hearts' focuses can then be shifted from own needs and onto their designed intentions. "Finally, brothers, whatever is true, whatever is honorable, whatever is just, whatever is pure, whatever is lovely, whatever is commendable, if there is any excellence, if there is anything worthy of praise, think about these things. What you have learned and received and heard and seen in me—practice these things, and the God of peace will be with you" (Philippians 4:8-9). Notice that the reward is peace, which is incidentally the companion of meek wisdom and the opposite of bitter jealousy and selfish ambition.

Reflection, Prayer and Action

- **Reflection**: Do you see jealousy, selfish ambition, disorder and sin in your life? Or do you see purity, peace, gentleness, reasonableness, mercy, progress, impartiality and sincerity? Write down three areas in which you have yet to see the results of godly wisdom.
- **Prayer**: "God, help me to hold onto your perfect wisdom, ready to give it the authority it deserves in my life. I want to walk away from the ways that I thought were best but ended up being broken in the end. Your wisdom is the ultimate standard in my life."
- **Action**: Look up the areas of your life that you wrote down before on www.openbible.info/topics or a similar Bible topic website or Bible. If you are struggling with staying sexually pure, type in "purity." If you are not seeing gentleness in your life, type in "gentleness." Read through the verses that appear and write down a few for each topic that seemed to jump out at you. Recite those verses out loud as part of your God-time routine and embrace the godly wisdom in each of them.

James Chapter 4

This chapter centers upon being redeemed, submitting to God's standard, and anchoring yourself to truth. There are some hard truths here, but we don't need to fear them or choke on them as long as we remember God's grace in each of them. We are desperately in need of God's assistance to successfully apply each of these magnificent processes.

James 4:1-10
Unrolling the Plan for Redemption

"What causes quarrels and what causes fights among you? Is it not this, that your passions are at war within you? You desire and do not have, so you murder. You covet and cannot obtain, so you fight and quarrel. You do not have, because you do not ask. You ask and do not receive, because you ask wrongly, to spend it on your passions. You adulterous people! Do you not know that friendship with the world is enmity with God? Therefore whoever wishes to be a friend of the world makes himself an enemy of God. Or do you suppose it is to no purpose that the Scripture says, 'He yearns jealously over the spirit that he has made to dwell in us'? But he gives more grace. Therefore it says, 'God opposes the proud, but gives grace to the humble.' Submit yourselves therefore to God. Resist the devil, and he will flee from you. Draw near to God, and he will draw near to you. Cleanse your hands, you sinners, and purify your hearts, you double-minded. Be wretched and mourn and weep. Let your laughter be turned to mourning and your joy to gloom. Humble yourselves before the Lord, and he will exalt you."

– James 4:1-10

"Do nothing from selfish ambition or conceit, but in humility count others more significant than yourselves. Let each of you look not only to his own interests, but also to the interests of others. Have this mind among yourselves, which is yours in Christ Jesus, who, though he was in the form of God, did not count equality with God a thing to be grasped, but emptied himself, by taking the form of a servant, being born in the likeness of men. And being found in human form, he humbled himself by becoming obedient to the point of death, even death on a cross. Therefore God has highly exalted him and bestowed on him the name that is above every name, so that at the name of Jesus every knee should bow, in heaven and on earth and under the earth, and every tongue confess that Jesus Christ is Lord, to the glory of God the Father."
– Philippians 2:3-11

"But godliness with contentment is great gain, for we brought nothing into the world, and we cannot take anything out of the world."
– 1 Timothy 6:6-7

Laying out the Plan

As a very amateur and inconsistent visitor of museums, I have two methods of studying paintings. I either stand very close to it to examine each intricate detail or I stand several feet away and examine what the painting means as a whole. If you are at all familiar with the works of Georges Seurat, viewing one of his paintings using the first approach can be rather confusing. As a pointillist, Seurat used dots rather than traditional brush strokes to create fascinating images of landscapes and people. I have had the pleasure of seeing some of his paintings in person and am particularly enchanted with *A Sunday Afternoon on the Island of La Grande Jatte*. When too closely examined, the combination of bold colors and tiny dots are interesting, but when the entire painting is viewed at a distance our imaginations are startled by Seurat's genius and creativity. Somehow the combination of seemingly unrelated colors and simple dots meld together to generate a harmony is generated that we would not have expected. If you can, go look at a high-resolution image of some of his paintings right now so you can see what I'm talking about.

In this same way, James constructed this section of his letter in such a way that the whole is greater than the sum of its parts. This is the great plan for continual reconciliation and freedom with God. Each topic is like a collection of dots that, by itself, is necessary but not the full picture. There is no way of neatly separating the various topics in this section of the letter without losing some of the total impact. All of it adds up to a cohesive plan in which multiple events happen simultaneously. I am compelled by the constraints of writing to tackle one element at a time to better explain each of them, but once you've finished reading this, I'd like to challenge you to read through verses 1 through 10 quickly multiple times, imagining that you are taking swift gulps of insight. By reading this, you will understand each individual color and shape better, but once you have done so, you will need to take a few steps back to see them all in unison.

Confront the Immensity of Your Sin

The first element of the plan of the plan of reconciliation and constant communion with God is to identify the vastness of our sin. Near the end of the last chapter, James touched a little bit on being peaceable instead of living with "disorder and every vile practice". Those thoughts seem to have triggered this particular section of James' writing in which he discusses the ramifications of our sinful nature. The bitter jealousy and selfish ambition that comes from earthly wisdom fuel the fire in which friendships, families and marriages are burned up. We see in this section that our passions are at war within us, and that we must respond to that war with the gospel.

The particular sins that James points to here are those that have to do with handling our resources (verses 1-3). The question of how to allocate money, time and other resources permeates almost every part of the Bible. It is especially visible in the Gospels when Jesus is discussing the use of money. It was important to Jesus that we know that we are to spend our resources wisely and not hoard foolishly (Matthew 25:14-30). It is fitting that James chose that topic to introduce us to our sin, seeing as it is among the most straightforwardly identifiable sins. The spotlight has now been focused on the way that we interact with what we have or don't have. Our responses concerning our circumstances are what make our actions sinful or righteous, not the circumstances themselves. We may discover that we have a desperate need in some area of our lives. When confronted with that reality, we can either make an appeal to God, trusting that he will come through, or we can chase after other sources of provision, which typically find their center our own abilities and strengths. A scarcity mindset then becomes our worldview and we are stuck in an endless cycle of fighting over scraps. Whatever the reasons for chasing after provision on our own, we are short-circuiting the process that we were designed work within. "You do not have, because you do not ask" (James 4:2b).

Alternatively, we may be in continual prayer about the things that we "need", but if we have our priorities wrong our prayers may be hampered. "You ask and do not receive, because you ask wrongly, to spend it on your passions" (James 4:2). In this case, we may have developed a "friendship with the world" in which we desire what the world has to offer more than what a relationship with God has to offer. This will make us into traitors against God because we would be serving the world's purposes that are contrary to God's plan. James, and many other authors of the Bible, defines this type of betrayal as an act of adultery and equates it to a spouse going off and fooling around with other people. As an example of this, we see that God commenced his relationship with the people of Israel as a proud bridegroom: "Go and proclaim in the hearing of Jerusalem, Thus says the Lord, 'I remember the devotion of your youth, your love as a bride, how you followed me in the wilderness, in a land not sown'" (Jeremiah 2:2). But the people became so wrapped up in their own desires that they longed to worship the gods of the people around them instead of the one who had already proven himself time and again to be the one true God. God, in his righteousness, had to separate himself from this unfaithful wife of a nation. "She saw that for all the adulteries of that faithless one, Israel, I had sent her away with a decree of divorce. Yet her treacherous sister Judah did not fear, but she too went and played the whore" (Jeremiah 3:8). Thankfully, even after this separation there is redemption upon redemption with God, and so he decided to join himself back with them even before he sent them away: "For this is the covenant that I will make with the house of Israel after those days, declares the LORD: I will put my law within them, and I will write it on their hearts. And I will be their God, and they shall be my people" (Jeremiah 31:33). You see that he did not simply make them love him, but instead wrote the law on their hearts. That way, they would have to confront their sins and go through the elements in this plan to be reconciled with God.

Because God is infinitely more concerned with our spiritual wellbeing than our comfort, he often chooses to keep us from receiving what we ask for with wrong motives, knowing that this will do no good for our souls. God, in his sovereignty, may answer the prayers of a person who is only centered on his own concerns, but that person's prayers will not be connected with the full power of God. I've caught myself red handed in this area, having slipped into a perspective where I invite God into my life and plans instead of seeking to understand and accept his life and plans. In those times, my concern was planted in my own passions, desires, feelings and thoughts rather than his glorious perspective. God does not ignore our prayers because he is proud; he holds off on fulfilling some of them because he knows that our souls will rot if he always feeds us the sugary delights that we demand. This situation is one of the main reasons why people who pray become disillusioned with God and prayer. By approaching God with a vending machine mindset, they misunderstand the whole purpose of prayer. Rather than asking God, "Where would you like to go?", they hop behind the wheel and yell over their shoulder, "Are you coming?" The relationship into which we were designed to fit becomes an exchange where perceived good acts are given to God with the expectation of getting something in return.

Don't misunderstand: Jesus taught us to pray for our immediate needs. He instructed us to pray, "Give us this day our daily bread" and he desires to answer that prayer (Matthew 6:11). However, before Jesus instructed us to pray for ourselves, he started his prayer template with, "Our Father in heaven, hallowed be your name" (Matthew 6:9b). The priority in this plan is to always to connect ourselves to God, as a wheel's hub to an axle (as we found in the last chapter concerning our words). If we do not identify the actions and thoughts that grieve God's heart, we will certainly succumb to prayers for God to fulfill our own cravings. Instead, we must be lifted up to where God is so we can observe the great factory of our hearts that has been producing sin our entire lives. Once you see that, you may be praying for the same things as you were when you were only looking at yourself, but in the new position, the reasons behind your prayer will probably be drastically different.

The movie *The Passion of the Christ* has been impactful to me in multiple ways. When I was watching it for the second time recently, I was impacted by the full gravity of my sin during the scene in which Jesus was being whipped. I sobbed heavily and buried my face in my hands. I experienced in that moment a glimpse of the enormity of my sin and the extent to which it grieves the Holy Spirit. I discerned a little bit about what James meant when he said, "[God] yearns jealously over the spirit he has made to dwell in us" (James 4:5). This jealousy is not the kind that flares up in the mind of a boy who sees someone flirting with the girl he likes. It is also not the kind of jealousy that a person has for his neighbor's brand-new sports car. Rather, God is filled with love for us and angered by the caustic effect that sin has on us. Instead of being jealous about us, God is jealous for us and our happiness. He is passionately desirous to see us happy. He actively pursues what he knows will make us joyful and destroys what would harm us. Like a father seeking to free his children from the grasp of a kidnapper, God is jealous for our wellbeing and will not stop until we are liberated. This jealousy is what inspired Jesus to give himself up for us.

Humble Yourself

Now that we have confronted the immensity of our sin, what shall we do? Dietrich Bonhoeffer, who was a celebrated Christian author, pastor, theologian and martyr, wrote a fascinating book titled *The Cost of Discipleship*. In this book, he discusses cheap grace, which is a concept that takes all of the goodness of God's grace that washes away our sin and then minimizes the immense price that God paid for it. He says, "Cheap grace is the grace we bestow on ourselves. Cheap grace is the preaching of forgiveness without requiring repentance, baptism without church discipline, Communion without confession… Cheap grace is grace without discipleship, grace without the cross, grace without Jesus Christ, living and incarnate."

In this second element of the plan, James uses the commands "submit", "humble", "be wretched", "mourn", "weep", and "cleanse your hands" to convey to us the methods by which we respond to our sin. Cheap grace would accept Jesus' gift of justification and forgiveness with a shrug, but recognition of the cost of grace produces an entirely different response. It does no good to confront your sin if you subsequently choose to cry about it but not do anything else. Confronting our sin is the first element, but it must be combined with a humility and submission to God that compliments the identification of our sin. This is meekness in action. As I mentioned briefly in the "Putting on Meekness" section of chapter 1, meekness is not weakness; it is our strength in submission to God's authority.

James gives to all of us imperative commands in verses 7-10 that give structure and definition to what it looks like to repent and turn from evil. These few verses direct us to the antidote for everything vile that James has mentioned so far and will mention later on: temptation, partiality, unbelief, inaction, quarreling, selfish ambition, jealousy, double-mindedness, boasting, covetousness, and the wickedness of our tongues. Let's look at how to apply this powerful anti-venom to our lives.

The repetition that we see of the words and actions that relate to humility was intentional. James was not just being wordy here. James is emphasizing both the importance of this element and the repetition that is required in this process. We cannot simply submit to God once and believe that we are forever in that posture before him. God certainly does not push us away, but our own hearts guide us away from the truth that he has for us and pulls us into a most dangerous position: Thinking that we are doing all right while not relying on God. As Jeremiah 17:9 says, "The heart is deceitful above all things, and desperately sick; who can understand it?" We must marry our humility with the steadfastness that we have been reading about.

An awareness of our sins married with a godly humility will lead us to look at our same needs in a new way. For example, instead of praying for a raise in order to buy something for yourself, you may be praying for more income to be able to give more to others. From the perch of our minds, it's simple to be duped into thinking that God doesn't have our best interests in mind. When we are sitting next to him, we can see that he will certainly take care of us. Our focus starts to shift outward to others and to God.

This is what the declaration of a man who is determined to be consistently humble looks like: "Let us also lay aside every weight, and sin which clings so closely, and let us run with endurance the race that is set before us…" (Hebrews 12:1). Paul - the writer of Hebrews - heard the call, felt the urgency, humbled himself, and bolted from his sin. No longer content to be stuck with his baggage, he threw it at the feet of Jesus. This ties in closely with what we're going to talk about next.

Resist the Devil

This third element is probably the least popular to discuss. Most of us, or at least I, don't like to feel like we've been manipulated by the devil or his demons. The culture in which we've grown up has portrayed evil as cartoon characters and fiction instead of the blood curdling reality that they are. This is why opening our minds up to a biblical understanding of the devil is a little complex. There are many mentions of the devil in the Bible, especially in the New Testament, and each one shows him as a threat. For anyone interested in understanding more about how the devil's schemes, I would highly recommend *The Screwtape Letters* by C.S. Lewis. Lewis wrote the book in the form of instructional letters from a veteran demon, Screwtape, to a novice demon. By hearing the diabolical perspective from the fictional Screwtape, we can hear teachings about resisting the devil in a new light and can see plainly how to resist him and his demons. I agree with his inference in that book that the devil's scheme in the last few hundred years has been centered on hiding himself and making himself seem to be nonexistent. Rather than manifesting in horrifying ways to frighten us into thinking that he is more powerful than us as he did in past centuries, his strategy in this culture is to remain camouflaged and resort to guerilla warfare tactics. This is damaging to us as we are less alert in identifying when he is attacking. We have been lulled into thinking that there is no war and therefore are caught off guard whenever a spiritual bombardment occurs.

Our resistance, as all actions of Christians, should not be based on our own skills or abilities but rather on our reliance on God. Do you see how these first three elements of the plan come together as one? Confronting your sin, humbling yourself, and resisting the devil are all aspects of the same process. We must resist the devil, but it is done through submission to Christ. However, being submitted to Christ without determinedly resisting the devil would not be effective either. "For though we walk in the flesh, we are not waging war according to the flesh. For the weapons of our warfare are not of the flesh but have divine power to destroy strongholds. We destroy arguments and every lofty opinion raised against the knowledge of God, and take every thought captive to obey Christ, being ready to punish every disobedience, when your obedience is complete" (2 Corinthians 10:3-6). As we see in this excerpt, our weapon is our thoughts in submission to God. The strongholds, lofty opinions, and thoughts mentioned all relate to the warfare of the mind rather than of physical obstacles. While physical issues can be daunting, we see from this section of James that our passions, pride, double-mindedness, covetousness, and wrong motives put us into real danger. These certainly stem from our broken nature, but they are inflamed by the work of the devil who "...prowls around like a roaring lion, seeking someone to devour" (1 Peter 5:8). When we dwell on a sinful action, he is more than happy to give us the extra incentive and lure us into his den so he can make a meal out of our misappropriated passions.

Run to God

As I said before, these elements are meant to occur simultaneously, so when I say that this is the last element, I do not mean it from a timing perspective but simply that I've chosen to talk about this one at the end. I decided to put it here because this one is my favorite. The three other pieces are essential, but this element involves God filling our emptiness and giving us purpose and joy.

This chapter starts off by identifying the warning signs that that make us aware of our spiritual sickness. God is righteous and we are wicked, stirring up his wrath. How does this tension get resolved in Christianity? It is grace that joins this together. Grace is the pivotal element of the gospel message and this entire chapter is permeated by it. The transforming power of grace is what leads us to the place where God exalts us because we have humbled ourselves in his grace. "But he gives more grace. Therefore it says, "God opposes the proud, but gives grace to the humble" (James 4:6). Without verse 6, verses 1-5 in this section become proclamations of hopelessness. Everything is lost without grace. When grace appears, we receive a glorious victory and a path to overwhelming joy. The road is not easy, but it is filled with hope. James doesn't begin this section with grace. Instead, he began it by highlighting our brokenness. He places grace right in the middle of calls to lay down our works and accept God's righteousness.

When we simultaneously confront our sin, humble ourselves, and resist the devil, we are putting ourselves in a rather precarious place if we do not run to God. If we rely on God's strength to apply the first three elements, we may be inclined to celebrate the great progress we've made and then not run wholeheartedly to God. If we think we're doing all right on our own steam, we may be tricked into thinking that we don't need God's help as much as we do. If we don't give God the chance to fill us up in his over-the-top way, we will be quickly crushed by the weight of one or more of the other elements of the plan. We were never meant to do this on our own strength.

> God made us: invented us as a man invents an engine. A car is made to run on petrol, and it would not run properly on anything else. Now God designed the human machine to run on Himself. He Himself is the fuel our spirits were designed to burn, or the food our spirits were designed to feed on. There is no other. That is why it is just no good asking God to make us happy in our own way without bothering about religion. God cannot give us a happiness and peace apart from Himself, because it is not there. (C.S. Lewis, *Mere Christianity*)

The Bible, especially when it comes to the Psalms, is permeated by the notion that God is approachable and loving. It is also filled with people who fall within two basic camps: Those who decided to do life under their own power and those who, whether consistently or not, ran to this loving God to receive help. Rather than going through every single story that proves this, I would like to instead point you back to the last phrase that James states in relation to this glorious plan: "Humble yourselves before the Lord, and he will exalt you." In the Message translation of the Bible, this phrase reads, "Get down on your knees before the Master; it's the only way you'll get on your feet." God's intention for this plan is not to make you feel guilty, cry, run scared from the devil, and crawl back to him. His intention is to help us to triumph over all the messy, hurtful things in our lives and put us on his shoulders. He wants to take a victory lap with us as his magnificent father's heart shouts joyfully about our conquest.

Reflection, Prayer and Action

- **Reflection**: How often do you intentionally confront your sin, humble yourself, resist the devil, and run to God? When you do, do you come out of the other side walking in freedom? If not, what part of the process are you getting hung up on?
- **Prayer**: "God, thank you for your forgiveness. I want to be rid of my sin and I know that it is only possible through your mercy. Help me to confront the immensity of my sin, humble myself, resist the devil, and sprint to your arms."
- **Action**: Block out some time today to spend 20-30 minutes to go through the process of redemption. Don't feel like you have to recite every sin you've ever knowingly or unknowingly committed. Instead, approach the situation by asking the Holy Spirit to reveal the sins you need to ask forgiveness for and believe that you have received the forgiveness.

James 4:11-12
Submitting to the Ultimate Standard

"[My] brethren, do not speak evil about or accuse one another. He that maligns a brother or judges his brother is maligning and criticizing the Law and judging the Law. But if you judge the Law, you are not a practicer of the Law but a censor and judge [of it]. One only is the Lawgiver and Judge Who is able to save and to destroy [the One Who has the absolute power of life and death]. [But you] who are you that [you presume to] pass judgment on your neighbor?"
– James 4:11-12 AMP

"Why do you pass judgment on your brother? Or you, why do you despise your brother? For we will all stand before the judgment seat of God; for it is written, 'As I live, says the Lord, every knee shall bow to me, and every tongue shall confess to God.' So then each of us will give an account of himself to God."
– Romans 14:10-12

Unfurling the Law

When I first read this section of James, I got the strange impression that it completely contradicted other places in the Bible that discuss how to identify good and confront evil in other Christians. It seemed as though James was forbidding us to follow even what Jesus said about conflict, which he outlined very clearly in this instance below:

> "If your brother sins against you, go and tell him his fault, between you and him alone. If he listens to you, you have gained your brother. But if he does not listen, take one or two others along with you, that every charge may be established by the evidence of two or three witnesses. If he refuses to listen to them, tell it to the church. And if he

refuses to listen even to the church, let him be to you as a Gentile and a tax collector." (Matthew 18:15-17)

For us to accurately understand what James is saying here, we have to look at it in context of Jesus' words. Once we do so, we will see that instead of contradiction, there is an agreement between the two.

In both instances, Jesus and James highlight the proper way to interact with "brothers". In the context of Christianity, they are referring to other Christians – both male and female – who are professing to be Christians and are progressively growing to be more like Christ. They are juxtaposing the relationship of "brother" we have with other Christians against the hostile attitudes that often flare up against one another.

Why didn't they say, "Interact with everyone this way"? Isn't that an example of James promoting partiality? Well, as we saw in James 2 in relation to compassion, these sorts of game-changing perspective shifts should always start with the Christians around us. To quote the same words I quoted from Jesus back in chapter 2, "A new commandment I give to you, that you love one another: just as I have loved you, you also are to love one another. By this all people will know that you are my disciples, if you have love for one another" (John 13:34). In other words, we serve everyone around us best when we focus a good portion of our energies on interacting well with other Christians. In this context, it means that we are to stop ourselves from speaking evil against them and judging them. But how do we do that practically?

Smear Job

Recently, I was listening to a podcast by Judah Smith, pastor of City Church in Seattle, about Paul's words in 1 Corinthians 13:7 concerning love, which reads, "Love bears all things, believes all things, hopes all things, endures all things." Smith broke it down into four main topics, the first being "Love bears all things". Explaining that the word "bear" in this phrase contains the same root word for "roof" in Greek. He described this act of bearing all things as protecting others so that they have the opportunity to work out their faults and sins in safety. This is opposed to the habit of speaking "evil against one another", which is gossip that zeroes in on the faults of others. What James is warning against here is waving around other people's dirty laundry.

When we humbly confront other Christians in their sins, we give them the opportunity to open up and show us their wounds. With a physical wound, you must first clean it, put salve on it, and then wrap it up to protect it from the elements. In Christ, we have the opportunity to work with the Holy Spirit to clean, anoint, and wrap up spiritual and emotional injuries. But, when we gossip, we are ripping open the bandages of Christians who are attempting to heal, which will hurt them and potentially damage our relationships with them.

I didn't grow up with a tendency toward gossip, but I have tasted its bewitching sweetness and can see how it could easily ensnare me if I let myself enjoy it. The draw of gossip becomes compounded when we consider how difficult it is to identify gossip. If we all reflect for a moment, we'll see that there seems to be a very blurry line between gossip and sharing information in attempt to get advice. Because it is not easily noticed, we can gossip under the guise of trying to help another person. I was very confused about how to articulate the difference until I heard of a great acid test to know whether I am about to gossip or not: Just ask yourself, "Is my motivation centered on helping the person I'm about to talk about?" This question helps us read our hearts and make the call. When I ask myself that question, I usually get a fast, hard "yes" or "no" in my spirit. If I am not sure, I abstain from sharing.

This question also aids in determining whether or not we should be sharing this information with the particular person or people we are with. You may have the best intentions, but if you know the people you are talking with consistently gossip, this question will raise a big red flag. If you know someone who shares a lot of other people's secrets with you, they will likely be sharing what you divulge with others. In the end, we serve others best when we do one of two things: Keep silent, or pure-heartedly seek the advice of trustworthy, helpful people.

On Trial

Those of us who have the privilege of bandaging someone spiritually or emotionally also must be wary of the propensity to judge the person we are helping. The other error that James warns us about here is judging others against our righteousness. I find this one particularly hard since the process through which we go to provide godly advice and correction travels within a stone's throw of judgment. If misappropriated, the discernment that God gives us so we can track down sin and destroy it can turn us into a fault-seeking bloodhound. Instead of using it to fight the enemy, it can be turned upon those who are being assaulted. We are to hate the sin and help the sinner get free.

Before I go further, I am compelled to discuss something that may appear to muddy the waters even further. Even though judging is forbidden in all other circumstances, as Christians we are commanded to judge other Christians by the fruit of their actions in order to protect Christianity. There are several prominent instances in the New Testament where people were excommunicated from the church because, though they claimed to be Christians, they were acting in a way that defamed the message of Christianity. We can distinguish this Christian judgment from the others in two ways: Firstly, the heart of this kind of judgment is to protect the sanctity of Christianity, not to punish. Secondly, it is never directed at those who do not profess to be Christians. Who are we to judge someone against a moral standard that they do not embrace? That is for God to judge. The only time where we must pass judgment is in confronting Christians in a holy way that is compelled to protect the name of Christ. With that distinction out of the way, let's examine the kinds of judgment that James is warning us against here.

Why do we feel compelled to override God's authority and places ourselves at the bench, raining down sentences with the gavel of our own righteousness? Our tendency to judge stems from a defense mechanism that reacts to our own sin and tries to mitigate its impact upon our minds and souls. Rather than mourning our sin and being comforted, as Jesus commands in the Beatitudes in Matthew 5, we divert the outrage we should feel about our own sin toward others. "Judge not, that you be not judged. For with the judgment you pronounce you will be judged, and with the measure you use it will be measured to you. Why do you see the speck that is in your brother's eye, but do not notice the log that is in your own eye? Or how can you say to your brother, 'Let me take the speck out of your eye,' when there is the log in your own eye? You hypocrite, first take the log out of your own eye, and then you will see clearly to take the speck out of your brother's eye" (Matthew 7:1-5).

Ironically, if we let ourselves continue in passive or active judging, we will likely be tempted to commit the same sorts of sins that we were judging in others. "Brothers, if anyone is caught in any transgression, you who are spiritual should restore him in a spirit of gentleness. Keep watch on yourself, lest you too be tempted. Bear one another's burdens, and so fulfill the law of Christ" (Galatians 6:1-2). Our fight against judging is also a fight that keeps temptation at bay.

The penchant that we have to judge is brought to its knees by active, ongoing forgiveness. "Put on then, as God's chosen ones, holy and beloved, compassionate hearts, kindness, humility, meekness, and patience, bearing with one another and, if one has a complaint against another, forgiving each other; as the Lord has forgiven you, so you also must forgive" (Colossians 3:12-13). If we let Jesus' compassion towards us permeate us, we will be inspired to be forgiving to others.

Give It Up

At their core, gossip and judging are avenues through which pride can come as a Trojan horse into our souls. Pride is essentially anti-God because it desires to tower over everyone else, including God. We do well to avoid it, and therefore must treat gossip and judging as cancerous. James goes so far as to say that our speaking evil about and judging each other are a direct assault upon the law which we were supposedly trying to defend. In a moment of self-righteousness, we may say something "in defense of the law" in a way that is directly opposed to the law. As we discussed in chapter 2, by disregarding the intent of the Law of Liberty with our thoughts and actions, we are in rebellion against the entirety of the law.

In his commentary on the book of James, John Calvin wrote:

> He then who rashly judges his brother; shakes off the yoke of God, for he submits not to the common rule of life. It is then an argument from what is contrary; because the keeping of the law is wholly different from this arrogance, when men ascribe to their conceit the power and authority of the law. It hence follows, that we then only keep the law, when we wholly depend on its teaching alone and do not otherwise distinguish between good and evil; for all the deeds and words of men ought to be regulated by it.

Like Calvin, all Christians come to the awareness that God is the ultimate lawgiver and judge. This truth is simple enough to say, but once we try to apply it to uncomfortable or challenging circumstances, reasons will appear for why our own opinions should trump God's commandments. When we examine our actions and thoughts, we often find a disturbing mixture of lust, anger, jealousy, covetousness, judging, gossip, dissatisfaction with God, and other sinful traits. What do we do then? When we know that we are inadequate, a common response is that of deflection. In James 4:1-10, we are called to humble ourselves before God and mourn our sin. Instead, we sometimes desire to punish the sin we find in others to abate our own gnawing realization that we are infested by sin.

Out of all of the statements that I've made concerning judging, this one is the quickest to adjust my perspective to where it ought to be: Each of us will one day be sitting in the docket awaiting the judgment of God. We will not be judges or even bailiffs in this holy courtroom. We are all equally guilty in the eyes of God without Jesus. For those of us who are Christian, we all await the same verdict: Blameless and righteous before God because of belief in Jesus. God, our just judge, is able to save and to destroy, but his actions are always righteousness and loving. His desire is to keep you from being tied up by your judging heart and blabbering mouth. We are decisively unqualified to be judges of others or share tidbits about other's sin. Among other things, we don't have the knowledge or authority to be impartial and just in our determinations. We are unfit to judge and have the responsibility to lay down the powdered wigs and robes we have made for ourselves and tell God, "I don't want your job. Please help me to trust you and obey you." When we do that, we find the freedom and ability to help others without laying on their shoulders the guilt we have in ourselves.

Reflection, Prayer and Action

- **Reflection**: Do you see the avenues of gossip and judging in your soul? Are they well trafficked paths?
- **Prayer**: "God, help me to spurn gossip and judging in my life. Instead, let me humbly confront other Christians with the intent to help them heal and grow closer to you."
- **Action**: Take a few extra seconds before you start to talk about someone this week. Think about the way that God has outlined for us to talk about others and compare what you are about to say against it. If it doesn't line up, say something else. If you see another Christian who needs to be confronted about their sin, pray about whether or not it should be you. If you're supposed to be the one confronting them, do it humbly and in private.

James 4:13-17
Anchoring Yourself

"Come now, you who say, 'Today or tomorrow we will go to such and such a city, and spend a year there and engage in business and make a profit.' Yet you do not know what your life will be like tomorrow. You are just a vapor that appears for a little while and then vanishes away. Instead, you ought to say, 'If the Lord wills, we will live and also do this or that.' But as it is, you boast in your arrogance; all such boasting is evil. Therefore, to one who knows the right thing to do and does not do it, to him it is sin."
– James 4:13-17 NASB

"He who disciplines the nations, does he not rebuke? He who teaches man knowledge— the Lord —knows the thoughts of man, that they are but a breath."
– Psalm 94:10-11

"Pray for us, for we are sure that we have a clear conscience, desiring to act honorably in all things."
– Hebrews 13:18

Be Here

In another quote from *The Screwtape* Letters, we get a glimpse outside of our usual perspective on time and eternity. In this section, Screwtape, the demon, explains to his protégée the function of the present in God's plan:

> The humans live in time but our Enemy [God] destines them to eternity. He therefore, I believe, wants them to attend chiefly to two things, to eternity itself, and to that point of time which they call the Present. For the Present is the point at which time touches eternity. Of the present moment, and of it only, humans have an experience analogous to the experience which our Enemy has of

> reality as a whole; in it alone freedom and actuality are offered them. He would therefore have them continually concerned either with eternity (which means being concerned with Him) or with the Present — either meditating on their eternal union with, or separation from, Himself, or else obeying the present voice of conscience, bearing the present cross, receiving the present grace, giving thanks for the present pleasure.

A few thoughts later, Screwtape explains why diverting our focus to the future presents so many opportunities for sin:

> In a word, the Future is, of all things, the thing least like eternity. It is the most completely temporal part of time — for the Past is frozen and no longer flows, and the Present is all lit up with eternal rays. Hence the encouragement we have given to all those schemes of thought such as Creative Evolution, Scientific Humanism, or Communism, which fix men's affections on the Future, on the very core of temporality. Hence nearly all vices are rooted in the future. Gratitude looks to the past and love to the present; fear, avarice, lust, and ambition look ahead.

How do we apply this understanding of time and single-mindedness? Firstly, we see from James' recommendation that our focus must remain on God no matter what. He declares, "...you ought to say, 'If the Lord wills...'" to emphasize the importance of God's will in our lives. Because we can only interact with God through the present, our thoughts, actions and motivations must reside there. Moving our focus primarily on the future and all of its fears and hopes causes us to lose the opportunity to let God handle the future. "But seek first the kingdom of God and his righteousness, and all these things will be added to you. Therefore do not be anxious about tomorrow, for tomorrow will be anxious for itself. Sufficient for the day is its own trouble" (Matthew 6:33-34).

Secondly, we must not be too attached to our plans, because we don't know what will happen tomorrow. Of course, we still ought to make plans for our lives. We see examples of this throughout the Bible, but all truly successful plans were always rooted in God. "Commit your work to the Lord, and your plans will be established…The heart of man plans his way, but the Lord establishes his steps" (Proverbs 16:3, 9).

Most of humanity has either not thought of this or has no concept of how to apply it to their lives. Being an action-oriented person, I consistently make the mistake of living in the future. Having a family, church, friends, job and home requires me to manage a rather large to-do list and schedule my time frugally. Even though I understand the concept that God desires us to operate under, my mind struggles to function in that way. I am regularly gnawed at by thoughts of the future and what it holds even after I have spent substantial time laying out the future in an organized and achievable way. Being a perfectionist, I never quite seem to get everything organized and nailed down the way I would like. Spending too much time attending to the future has cultivated unhealthy obsessions whenever I am not intentional in cutting back.

Another few thoughts after the last quote from *The Screwtape Letters*, the author presents God's desired method for using the present to plan the future:

> His [God's] ideal is a man who, having worked all day for the good of posterity (if that is his vocation), washes his mind of the whole subject, commits the issue to Heaven, and returns at once to the patience or gratitude demanded by the moment that is passing over him.

In other words, our focus on the future should be limited to actions that we can perform in the present. We can and ought to create plans, manage to-do lists and schedule our calendars in advance. God encouraged his people many times to do something that would take planning, effort and time. However, if we have three things to do today and five things to do tomorrow, we ought to concentrate on the three things and leave off thinking about the five things until tomorrow. If we must prepare for the five things today, we ought to prepare, but our attention should be limited to the required preparation for today and not on the potential successes and failures we may be met with tomorrow.

That being said, we must know when to stop planning and preparing. As I mentioned, I have an unhealthy desire to bring perfection to my to-do list and calendar. I can easily convince myself that what I'm doing is required, so I have to return to God and ask him for wisdom on whether or not to continue organizing.

You may not be in the same boat as me, but perhaps your heart is constantly skirmishing with a scarcity mentality. Or maybe you deeply desire a spouse and spend more time than you know you ought to obsessing over who it will be and what they will do for you. Or maybe you are saddled with an addiction to pornography or sex that, if you're honest with yourself, is only motivated by thoughts of the next sexual encounter or erotic video. If none of these apply, you can probably still identify another area of your life in which you are giving yourself to the future at the cost of the present.

All true pleasures in God are found in doing things here and now. Even those things that we do only because of the future rewards that God will give us have their motivation grounded in pleasing God in the present. If you know that you aren't residing in the present, spend some time writing down the areas of your life that you haven't been able to get control over. Then ask God to give you the strength and humility to lay down your fear, lust, ambition and anger, substituting them for a single-minded devotion to God through the present.

Turning a Blind Eye

In a strange way, the last thought in this section made me think about a background character in the movie *It's a Wonderful Life*. In this movie, a hard-working and worn-down soul named George Bailey battles to keep a town from being absorbed by an opportunist businessman of "Ebenezer Scrooge"-proportions named Potter. When everything finally seems to be going well for George and the town, one of George's colleagues accidentally gives a massive amount of his business' cash to Potter. Upon discovery, Potter quickly commands the employee pushing his wheelchair to wheel him up to a place where he can watch George's colleague frantically searching for the money. Knowing that this will enable him to finally crush George's building and loan business, he gloats in his office waiting for Mr. Bailey to come crawling to him for help.

Throughout the movie, Potter is obviously the villain, but when I thought about the movie recently I was struck by how Potter's employee mutely accepted the treacherousness of Potter's actions. Even at the end of the movie, no one but the audience knows about Potter's evil action or his employee's equally evil inaction. He could have called the police or even secretly taken the money back from Potter and given it to George. Instead, he stands silently in the top-left corner of the screen and his inaction is forgotten.

Dietrich Bonhoeffer left this chilling sentence for us to reflect upon: "Silence in the face of evil is evil." This perspective cuts down to the motivations of our hearts and can be an even surer test of our purity and righteousness than the actions that surface from our intentions. The question demands an answer that we may be ashamed to give.

Whether we held back from an appropriate time to talk about Jesus, neglected to help someone we knew was in need, or avoided being friendly to someone we have had a hard time with, our inaction may be camouflaged. Our inaction is usually not met with reproof by those around us because it is something that only we know about. If we aren't accountable to someone and honest with God about it, we may let hundreds of opportunities to do good slip by. As John Stuart Mill put it, "Bad men need nothing more to compass their ends, than that good men should look on and do nothing."

Our main objective then is to marry what we know about inaction with living in the present. Our reasons for not taking action may be that we would feel awkward, embarrassed, scared, too busy, angered, or any number of other emotions. However, if we treat every moment as if it is the only one we have control over (which is the truth), our paradigm shifts and we see the action as it is without the burden of the future. Rather than letting what's next dominate our perspectives, we examine the opportunities of each moment against the overall purpose that God has for our lives and make the call.

This truth is volatile. Those who accept it without operating from grace towards themselves and others will walk straight into the minefield of legalism. A person who operates from a legalistic spirit demands perfection from others even though he knows that he cannot perform perfectly himself. Spiteful people can turn James' righteous warning against inaction into a legalistic weapon. This connects back to the last section on judging others.

Alternatively, this warning can become a pit of despair. Since the first time I read this section of James, I flaked out of many chances to do the right things and then became racked with guilt over not having done them. I was deeply remorseful for not stopping for a person who obviously could have used a car ride, giving assistance to someone in need, or even introducing myself to someone who I could tell was feeling uncomfortable or alone. The Holy Spirit was the one encouraging me to do those things and I chickened out. What I did after that was either defined by grace or legalism. Some of the times, I acknowledged my weakness and asked God to give me strength to react more quickly and with greater compassion. In other words, I operated from under grace and turned to God for forgiveness and assistance. Other times, my focus was pulled inward to the badness that I found in myself wallowing secretly in shame and condemnation. I didn't reach out to God but instead resorted to self-deprecation to try to pay for my sins.

James did not intend to encourage legalism or despair, but rather to encourage us to always examine our hearts and our actions to determine if they line up with God's desires. When we find that we do not measure up to God, we must respond with repentance and receive his grace.

JAMES 4:13-17

Reflection, Prayer and Action

- **Reflection**: Do you live almost entirely focused on the future? Or are you anchored in the present? Were there times recently where you turned a blind eye to some evil?
- **Prayer**: "God, help me to live in the present, only thinking about the future long enough to make plans for it now. Let me to be aware of the evil going on around me. Keep me from turning a blind eye to it. I pray that I would be a person of action who is always ready to do the right thing."
- **Action**: Examine your thoughts throughout the day. If you find yourself unnecessarily focused on the future, bring your mind back to what you can do about it now, or just turn your mind to something else. If you see evil happening around you, confront it if possible and pray for God's kingdom to come into that situation.

James Chapter 5

This chapter signals the final lap of our adventure. The checkered flag is out and James is about to whip through the last challenges he has for us. It starts with a harsh deposition and transitions into comforting exhortations to receive and give healing, deliverance, patience and redemption. These concepts will equip us to better tackle the trials laid out in the last four chapters and bring us to triumphant victory in Christ.

JAMES 5:1-6
SHUNNING GREED

"Come now, you rich, weep and howl for the miseries that are coming upon you. Your riches have rotted and your garments are moth-eaten. Your gold and silver have corroded, and their corrosion will be evidence against you and will eat your flesh like fire. You have laid up treasure in the last days. Behold, the wages of the laborers who mowed your fields, which you kept back by fraud, are crying out against you, and the cries of the harvesters have reached the ears of the Lord of hosts. You have lived on the earth in luxury and in self-indulgence. You have fattened your hearts in a day of slaughter. You have condemned and murdered the righteous person. He does not resist you."
– James 5:1-6

"Man wastes away like a rotten thing, like a garment that is moth-eaten. Man who is born of a woman is few of days and full of trouble. He comes out like a flower and withers; he flees like a shadow and continues not."
– Job 13:28, 14:1-2

"Those who survive him the pestilence buries, and his widows do not weep. Though he heap up silver like dust, and pile up clothing like clay, he may pile it up, but the righteous will wear it, and the innocent will divide the silver."
– Job 27:15-17

Finding Greed

In James 1:10, having briefly exhorted the general population of rich people to be content in God, the author circles back and blasts the rich in this section. The rest of this letter follows a format of warning against some evil action followed by encouragements to change from evil to good. In this most scathing part of his letter, James rips into the rich with zealousness that doesn't seem to have any element of encouragement to turn from evil. This may seem uncharacteristically - and even unbiblically - devoid of grace, but we will examine why James approached this in such a sharp manner.

As I mentioned in the first chapter, this is not an indiscriminate rant against affluent people in general. After using the first few phrases to get their attentions by pointing out the results of their greed, he gets down to the details of how they got there. These verses are not meant to hack away at every prosperous person on the planet; there are many wealthy Christians who are wholeheartedly advancing God's kingdom. James' target audience is those who, like Ebenezer Scrooge at the beginning of *A Christmas Carol*, found no greater joy than in the accumulation of wealth at the expense of others. Regrettably, each and every one of us, regardless of what our bank account says, can be Scrooges in one or more areas of our lives. Don't leave this section without a healthy gut-check to see if you need to deal with a measure of greed in your life.

Greed and All of Its Friends

Before we dive into the ways that greed acts, let's examine the roots of greed. In his first shot across the bow of the greedy, James claims that the greedy have "laid up treasure in the last days." In this case, the treasure relates to material gain or anything that can be horded. These are the people who have gained more than they need but are unwilling to give a portion of the excess to those in need.

What does he mean by "last days"? There are various understandings of this. Firstly, the early Christians believed that God was going to come back in a very short time, so it's possible that James may have meant that. The "last days" also can refer to the time period right before the end of the world that is most thoroughly discussed in the book of Revelation. However, having just discussed the vapor-like timeframe of the human soul a few lines ago, it is more likely that the "last days" that James is referring relate to the certainty and proximity of our own deaths and subsequent judgment. In the New Living Translation, this phrase is translated this way: "This treasure you have accumulated will stand as evidence against you on the day of judgment" (James 5:3b NLT). In The Message translation, the focus of the phrase becomes even clearer: "You thought you were piling up wealth. What you've piled up is judgment" (James 5:3b MSG).

Rather than only obsessing over the timeframe of the "last days" or "end times" are, we ought to be preparing for our upcoming Judgment Day. It will be here before we know it and we should be ready to stand before God without a mountain of rotting, burning treasure to judge us.

How do we do that? Well, let's examine the symptoms that characterize greedy people. The greedy, stingy and corrupt rich in this passage are those that do not attend to what Jesus said in Matthew 10:28:

> And do not fear those who kill the body but cannot kill the soul. Rather fear him who can destroy both soul and body in hell.

In Job 27:16-19 we see a similar warning:

> ...though he heap up silver like dust, and pile up clothing like clay, he may pile it up, but the righteous will wear it, and the innocent will divide the silver. He builds his house like a moth's, like a booth that a watchman makes. He goes to bed rich, but will do so no more; he opens his eyes, and his wealth is gone.

We know from James chapter 2 that our works are outward evidence of our inward thoughts. In the momentary lives we have, we are faced with choices every day that test our priorities.

Money is an obvious first choice as it can be an enabler to the rest of the roots of greed. It is also the most recognizable form in our culture. Jesus explicitly dealt with money on many occasions. One that is most applicable to this section is this quote: "No one can serve two masters, for either he will hate the one and love the other, or he will be devoted to the one and despise the other. You cannot serve God and money" (Matthew 6:24). Rather than requiring a complete rejection of money, Jesus was stating the importance of the orienting our lives around him rather than on gathering material wealth.

Though the rest of these variations of greed may be less frowned upon in our culture, they are still just as sinful as the greed for money. This flavor of greed demands things be done perfectly and immediately, regardless of the toll it takes on others or on ourselves. Perfectionism often gets entangled with control, which places value in being able to manipulate and command others. Rather than just desiring perfection in its surroundings, power requires that others be under its thumb. The amassing of power and control is greed at its most dangerous.

There are many other strands of greed, but at their core all of these roots are fastened to the soil of impatience or pride. They gain their strength from our fears, lusts and self-absorption. Ultimately, James and many other parts of the Bible are warning us against making decisions that do not take God's eternal priorities into account. No matter what variation of greed you encounter or experience in yourself, it all stems from leaving God out of the equation.

Unjust Gain

James apparently had observed certain rich people hiring staff to perform work and then not paying them what they deserved. It's possible that this matter was brought before him in his duties as a pastor. We don't know whether these rich people held back the entire amount or part of it, but the workers needed their wages and became aware of the fraud because they cried out to God against the injustice.

We can see from the surrounding text that the motivation for withholding the money was probably to spend it on amenities and pleasure. Instead of keeping the money merely to provide for his basic needs - which would still be sinful - this man did so in order to cushion his already comfortable life. This section directly relates to the passage below in Deuteronomy:

> You shall not oppress a hired worker who is poor and needy, whether he is one of your brothers or one of the sojourners who are in your land within your towns. You shall give him his wages on the same day, before the sun sets (for he is poor and counts on it), lest he cry against

you to the Lord, and you be guilty of sin. (Deuteronomy 24:14-15)

In his commentary on the Letter of James, John Calvin discusses the futility and absurdity of gathering wealth for the sake of being wealthy:

> It is, indeed, true that those rich men are insane who glory in things so fading as garments, gold, silver, and such things, since it is nothing else than to make their glory subject to rust and moths... what [James] condemns here is the extreme rapacity of the rich, in retaining everything they could lay hold on, that it might rot uselessly in their chests. For thus it was, that what God had created for the use of men, they destroyed, as though they were the enemies of mankind.

The Sons of Korah help us recognize the brevity of our lives and the fading of riches in Psalm 49:16-20:

> Be not afraid when a man becomes rich, when the glory of his house increases. For when he dies he will carry nothing away; his glory will not go down after him. For though, while he lives, he counts himself blessed —and though you get praise when you do well for yourself— his soul will go to the generation of his fathers, who will never again see light. Man in his pomp yet without understanding is like the beasts that perish.

In the process of unjustly gathering wealth, a person incurs the wrath of God. As we see in verse 4, "the cries of the harvesters have reached the ears of the Lord of hosts." Contrary to the way you may read this, God was not previously unaware of the evil done against the hires. Rather, the language being used infers that God is already planning justice. Once a righteous king heard about a wrong being done, he moved into justice mode and prepared a way for judgment to be executed in the situation reported to him. The essence of this statement is that God is not deaf to pleas for justice in the world. God is referred to as the Lord of hosts, which is a term used to remind us of the incredible power and authority backing up the justice that will come. In our discussion of James

5:7-12 we will see that not all wrongs will be righted when we want them to be. Instead, we are to endure in patience until the time for justice has ripened. I know that I would prefer to have everything made perfect now, but I also am coming to understand that God's understanding is far above me and he will bring justice when it is the perfect time.

Is there some area of your life that you're holding back money, time or energy that someone deserves or needs? Does your family need you to step up to the plate and do something but you're procrastinating? Are you avoiding serving in the church because you are hoarding your time? Are you only giving the bare minimum at work? These are all examples of unjust gain in one form or another. The difficulty is that these forms of greed and unjust gain are not always easy to recognize in ourselves. Take some time today to wrestle with your motivations and see where you are giving less than you should in order to amass more money, time or energy for reasons that don't revolve around love and freedom.

Greed and Death

The vivid language used in James 5:5 paints a scarlet warning: "You have lived on the earth in luxury and in self-indulgence. You have fattened your hearts in a day of slaughter." In the New Living Translation the second-half of the verse reads: "You have fattened yourselves for the day of slaughter." As I was comparing the two versions, I saw two pictures simultaneously concerning the phrases "in a day of slaughter" and "for a day of slaughter".

When I read the phrase "in a day of slaughter", I am reminded of all of the stories I've heard of that have occurred during genocides, revolutions and wars where a select few people are gluttonously feeding off of the carnage and destruction around them. Primarily, the destruction is happening to everyone else and they are riding high.

In a memorable example of this, Roman Caesar Nero had been negligent with many aspects of his empire and so incurred the dissatisfaction of the people. The greed for power that he had made the needs of Rome grow dim while he fattened his heart. Because of a lack of necessary infrastructure, a fire that could have been stopped instead raged through a large portion of Rome, killing many people. Because of his deadened heart, he had no desire to take on the responsibility for his inaction, so he blamed the destructive fire on Christians, even thought it was due to his negligence concerning the city. He sanctioned the mass execution of Christians by crucifixion, mauling, and even turned some of them into human torches for their amusement. Nero did all this because he wanted to maintain and gain more power, regardless of what lies he had to make. This caused a mass exodus of Christians from Rome and generated persecution for the Roman church.

So that's the way I look at the words "in a day of slaughter". When I hear the words "For the day of slaughter", a different picture comes to mind. In this image I see that the things that were hoarded became the noose with which the greedy are hung. The perspective changes from profiting from the misfortunes of others to the viewpoint that greed will eventually ensure the destruction of the greedy. This thought lines up directly with the words of God in Ezekiel 7:19:

> They cast their silver into the streets, and their gold is like an unclean thing. Their silver and gold are not able to deliver them in the day of the wrath of the Lord. They cannot satisfy their hunger or fill their stomachs with it. For it was the stumbling block of their iniquity.

It also the correlates with Jeremiah 51:58:

> Thus says the Lord of hosts: The broad wall of Babylon shall be leveled to the ground, and her high gates shall be burned with fire. The peoples labor for nothing, and the nations weary themselves only for fire.

As a less extreme example, the church in Laodicea during the time of the early church was dealing with the issue of riches that was starting to deaden in their souls. John, the writer of the Book of Revelation, conveys this message from Jesus to his church:

> I know your works: you are neither cold nor hot. Would that you were either cold or hot! So, because you are lukewarm, and neither hot nor cold, I will spit you out of my mouth. For you say, I am rich, I have prospered, and I need nothing, not realizing that you are wretched, pitiable,

poor, blind, and naked. I counsel you to buy from me gold refined by fire, so that you may be rich, and white garments so that you may clothe yourself and the shame of your nakedness may not be seen, and salve to anoint your eyes, so that you may see. (Revelation 3:15-18)

Even though this was written to a specific church centuries ago, it is still applicable today. The church of Laodicea was lukewarm and lived a passive "Christian" life, neither burning for God nor completely turning away from him. This state is despicable to God as it shows that they were satisfied with mere reflections of him instead of his entire glory. They tasted of God and did not savor him. They worshiped God with half their hearts while the rest was consumed with selfishness and earthly pleasures. They saw themselves as rich and, in doing so, condemned themselves.

If we consciously or unconsciously declare our own self-sufficiency in any area of our lives, we shut off opportunities for blessing and grace. The result is that we can seek protection and security by barricading the door to our lives, thinking that we will be protected. However, that would just lead to being eaten alive by the corruption we have invited in with the intention of nourishing our souls.

James' challenge to all Christians is to stop playing spiritual games and become truly invested in finding all of our pleasure in God. Let us purge our hearts of any desires that do not originate in God and allow him to fill the emptiness with his supreme reign. What he desires for us is to be rich with "gold refined by fire," that is, eternal wealth in our souls and rewards for our good deeds. If you identify that you're treating any room in your heart like a bomb shelter "just in case", give it over to God and remember that he is the only permanent refuge. He will not fail you and he desires what's best for you.

Greed Mistreats Others

In his masterpiece titled *Mere Christianity*, C. S. Lewis, the great writer and theologian, identified a pattern in humanity that is both shocking and revealing: "When a man is getting better he understands more and more clearly the evil that is still left in him. When a man is getting worse he understands his own badness less and less." At this point in the first section of James 5, we have reached the depths of depravity in the heart of the greed. Their ability to identify evil has been absorbed by the black hole of their hearts. Rising to the occasion, James gets even more intense in the last verse of this section where he says, "You have condemned and murdered the righteous person. He does not resist you" (James 5:6). At this point, we see the height of greed's tyranny. Rather than only withholding good things from others, this glutinous greed seeks to absorb the good things that others have for no other reason than to crush them. Again, James does not present a positive exhortation for the greedy in this section. However, the wording that he uses will be helpful for those who are being bombarded by actions of aggressive greed.

Firstly, we see that a righteous person does not resist evil. Why is that? In Matthew 5:38-39, Jesus states, "You have heard that it was said, 'An eye for an eye and a tooth for a tooth.' But I say to you, Do not resist the one who is evil. But if anyone slaps you on the right cheek, turn to him the other also." This expression by Jesus is among the most baffling and difficult teachings that he expressed, unless you take it in context. Right after Jesus discussed retaliation, he discussed love by saying, "But I say to you, Love your enemies and pray for those who persecute you, so that you may be sons of your Father who is in heaven. For he makes his sun rise on the evil and on the good, and sends rain on the just and on the unjust" (Matthew 5:44-45).

Rather than being an instruction to play possum and let others run us over, what this tells me is that we ought to be willing to be overcome by suffering if it means that godly love prevails. In extreme examples, this shows itself in stories of martyrs who did not resist being killed because they knew that it was God's desire to show his love to their murderers. In a more every-day example, this may be that you act in grace toward those who cut you off on the road or in line at the grocery store. Or maybe you hold your tongue when someone hurls an insult directly at an injured part of your soul. Maybe someone boldly steals from you but you hear clearly from God to let it go. Regardless of the situation, this verse is a reminder that love takes precedence.

The second meaning of James 5:6 is that greedy people target those who are unable to resist their attacks. In the last chapter, we found that covetousness towards what others have can lead to fights, quarreling and even physical murder: "You desire and do not have, so you murder. You covet and cannot obtain, so you fight and quarrel. You do not have, because you do not ask" (James 4:2). Clearly, greedy covetousness can drive us to such passion for something that we would be willing to commit murder for it. Though that may seem to be a far-fetched situation, it doesn't start off that way. Instead, it is a slow process of sinking deeper into desire and further from trusting that God will provide for our needs. In place of praying for God to reposition our hearts in his, our course becomes set toward our fickle hearts. When that happens, we will find fleeting enjoyment followed by an eternal, endless search for happiness.

On top of being an eventually fruitless effort, stealing from others just because of pride further exacerbates the situation of the greedy because their cruelty is directed toward those who God promised he would protect. Back in James' day, this would have most likely meant widows, orphans, cripples, and anyone who was poor. Today, this group would also involve preying on desperate and insecure people through Internet scams, pyramid schemes and clever advertising. Throughout the Old and New Testaments, God promised that he would protect and come to the rescue of those who were poor, either spiritually or physically.

To expound upon our understanding of this type of prideful greediness, we go to the Psalms. Asaph, the song writer, observed this evil and expressed his reaction to it in vivid detail:

> For I was envious of the arrogant when I saw the prosperity of the wicked. For they have no pangs until death; their bodies are fat and sleek. They are not in trouble as others are; they are not stricken like the rest of mankind. Therefore pride is their necklace; violence covers them as a garment. Their eyes swell out through fatness; their hearts overflow with follies. They scoff and speak with malice; loftily they threaten oppression. (Psalm 73:3-8)

As an onlooker, Asaph was deeply affected by what seemed to be the free reign of greed and its associated terrors. He goes on for several more verses bemoaning the prosperity of the wicked people he observed. His tone dramatically changes when he encounters God's perspective on the matter:

> But when I thought how to understand this, it seemed to me a wearisome task, until I went into the sanctuary of God; then I discerned their end. (Psalm 73:16-17)

It was only when he discussed this matter with God that he was brought to realize the short-lived and meaningless successes of the covetous people around him.

We all have a savage dictator in us that yearns to live the "good life", absorbing the lives of others to gratify others. It is inevitable that whenever we do that on any scale, we are simultaneously preparing ourselves to be ruined in this life or, if not repented of, in eternity.

Asaph's epiphany is brought to full light in the last thought in this song:

> For behold, those who are far from you shall perish; you put an end to everyone who is unfaithful to you. But for me it is good to be near God; I have made the Lord God my refuge, that I may tell of all your works. (Psalm 73:27-28)

In one of the many memorable quotes from *Mere Christianity*, C.S. Lewis wrote, "For pride is spiritual cancer: it eats up the very possibility of love, or contentment, or even common sense." Truly, prideful greed is one of the most caustic and harsh environments for any soul. May we all avoid it and run to God, who is joyfully healing many who have this sickness rooted in their hearts.

Lose It, Gain It

While the subjects of James' tirade concerning greed may have been too far gone to hear a call to redemption, each one of us probably has traits and tendencies that could lead us down the same path of greed if we are not vigilant. With an assortment of greed waiting to trap us, we must be careful not to run away from one just to fall into another. Thankfully, even though there are many opportunities for failure, the solution for all of them is the same. To understand this, we again turn to the teachings of Jesus:

> The kingdom of heaven is like treasure hidden in a field, which a man found and covered up. Then in his joy he goes and sells all that he has and buys that field (Matthew 13:44).

In other words, to conquer greed we must seek to experience a far greater joy that overshadows the pleasures of gathering, hoarding, and oppressing others. What Jesus is encouraging us to do is invest all of our personal and spiritual capital in the Bank of God and let him manage the returns it will bring. This paradigm places God at the helm of our decision-making process and puts us happily in the place of obedient servant. Instead of spending all our time in fear of not having enough, we trust that God will come through with the resources that he promised.

Too often, I confuse my desire for comfort with God's guidance. It's easy to feel pulled in a direction that feels nicer and think that it is God guiding you to it. But as we hone our spiritual senses to hear God more clearly, we find that the voice of comfort has a different tone than God's. His tone has within it the sentiment that Paul provided to Timothy in his first letter to him:

> But godliness with contentment is great gain, for we brought nothing into the world, and we cannot take anything out of the world. But if we have food and clothing, with these we will be content (1 Timothy 6:6-8).

The Message translation of those same three verses drives the idea home:

> A devout life does bring wealth, but it's the rich simplicity of being yourself before God. Since we entered the world penniless and will leave it penniless, if we have bread on the table and shoes on our feet, that's enough.

I acknowledge that the sentiments in this segment may seem to be either difficult to swallow or boring and cliché, and I understand both angles. It is hard to stomach the idea that we need to give God control over everything. It is also an idea that has been expressed in numerous ways in church almost every Sunday, and some of us are tired of hearing about it. Whether you see this exhortation as almost impossible to embrace or you just wish we would talk about something else, my answer is the same: This next group of verses is just what we need.

Reflection, Prayer and Action

- **Reflection**: What is at the center of your priorities? Do you see the tendencies of greed in your heart? Have you been getting unjust gain in some area of your life?
- **Prayer**: "God, make me into the kind of person who always seeks your treasure above all else. Help me to have a healthy appreciation for the value of money, but let it be subordinated to the eternal value I find in you."
- **Action**: Give something away this week, whether it is time, money or energy. Go out of your way to bless others. If you have been getting unjust gain, approach the person or people you have been getting it from and ask for their forgiveness. Above all, take time to find your ultimate enjoyment in God today. Pray, read your Bible, and sing worship songs that talk about how wonderful God is.

James 5:7-12
Embracing Patience

"Be patient, therefore, brothers, until the coming of the Lord. See how the farmer waits for the precious fruit of the earth, being patient about it, until it receives the early and the late rains. You also, be patient. Establish your hearts, for the coming of the Lord is at hand. Do not grumble against one another, brothers, so that you may not be judged; behold, the Judge is standing at the door. As an example of suffering and patience, brothers, take the prophets who spoke in the name of the Lord. Behold, we consider those blessed who remained steadfast. You have heard of the steadfastness of Job, and you have seen the purpose of the Lord, how the Lord is compassionate and merciful. But above all, my brothers, do not swear, either by heaven or by earth or by any other oath, but let your 'yes' be yes and your 'no' be no, so that you may not fall under condemnation."
– James 5:7-12

"Be still before the Lord and wait patiently for him; fret not yourself over the one who prospers in his way, over the man who carries out evil devices! Refrain from anger, and forsake wrath! Fret not yourself; it tends only to evil. For the evildoers shall be cut off, but those who wait for the Lord shall inherit the land."
– Psalm 37:7-9

"Patience is bitter, but its fruit is sweet."
– Aristotle

The Magnificent Alternative to Greed

After the rather feisty few verses at the beginning of this chapter, James turns from the greedy, looks at those with him in Christ, and begins a gentle and firm appeal to us to flee from greed and become sanctified daily through patient endurance.

Patient endurance is illustrated well in a scene taken from the book titled *The Pilgrim's Progress* where two characters named Interpreter and Christian discuss the thoughts and actions of two other characters named Patience and Passion:

> Interpreter: So he said, These two lads are figures: Passion, of the men of this world; and Patience, of the men of that which is to come; for as here thou seest, Passion will have all now this year, that is to say, in this world; so are the men of this world, they must have all their good things now, they cannot stay till next year, that is until the next world, for their portion of good. That proverb, 'A bird in the hand is worth two in the bush', is of more authority with them than are all the Divine testimonies of the good of the world to come. But as thou sawest that he had quickly lavished all away, and had presently left him nothing but rags; so will it be with all such men at the end of this world.
>
> Christian: Then said Christian, Now I see that Patience has the best wisdom, and that upon many accounts. First, because he stays for the best things. Second, and also because he will have the glory of his, when the other has nothing but rags.

In other words, Christian came to the realization that Passion desires to have everything instantly and pays dearly for it in the end, whereas Patience sees what is most valuable and "stays for the best things." When we have patience, we embrace the waiting game, knowing that greed, impatience and passion will not satisfy our desire for God. Our patience works to supplant temporary delights with eternal joy that can start now.

Awaiting Judgment

We discussed judgment briefly back in James 4:11-12, but now I want to discuss an additional two flavors of judgment that pertain to this section. Our perception of judgment is an essential element in sustaining patience, so let's take some time to examine judgment.

In James 4, the type of judgment that was discussed mostly pertained to looking down on others and making judgment calls concerning others. Another reason to pass judgment on another person is if their sin directly affects us, either because the sin hurt us or someone we care about. Rather than just not looking down on that person, we have to deal with an extra layer of difficulty in withholding judging because it is a sin that has harmed us directly. In this case, judging can extend beyond looking down on someone to actively seeking to harm him or her emotionally or physically. In essence, we are mounting the steps of the courtroom bench, raining down sentences upon the person, then seeking to carry out those sentences to the best of our ability. This active judgment is expressly forbidden in the Bible. "Beloved, never avenge yourselves, but leave it to the wrath of God, for it is written, 'Vengeance is mine, I will repay, says the Lord.' To the contrary, 'if your enemy is hungry, feed him; if he is thirsty, give him something to drink; for by so doing you will heap burning coals on his head.' Do not be overcome by evil, but overcome evil with good" (Romans 12:19-21).

Whether active judgment is present or not, many of us will find that we are consumed by acidic, negative thoughts about the person who sinned against us.. This is one of the most common and heart wrenching ways that judgment manifests itself. Rather than choosing to fix the situation and forgive the person, we obsess over the wrong done to us and wallow in our hurt. Because it is what our hearts become centered on, our thoughts, actions and lifestyle begin to ooze with our grudge. This does nothing but nurse our festering pride and spew toxicity in every direction.

Active judgment and stewing over the wrongs done to us are both rooted in the absence of patience and understanding of true judgment. God's righteous judgment is the only valid reason to keep from taking revenge. The only reason not to retaliate is that God will repay all evil in a just way. If we know that only God can repay evil the way it deserves and in a just way, we are relieved from the tension that we feel when we see injustice occurring. We should still do the best we can to help right the wrongs that we see, but vengeance and judgment lay outside of our jurisdiction. We should not grumble against each other, knowing that the bad things that our fellow Christians do will be dealt with in a much better way than we ever could.

Examples of Patience

Now that we know that we should be patient, who are our role models? I would certainly not have been one of them as a kid. I was the antithesis of patience, particularly when it came to Christmas presents. While I still get enthusiastic on Christmas mornings, I used to have an all-consuming passion about finding out what was underneath the shiny wrapping paper and little note that said, "To Everett". For at least one Christmas, I was so incredibly eager to find out what I was going to get that I snuck into my parent's closet to get a peak at my gifts. My mom ended up catching me red-handed as I looked up at her sheepishly from the throne of presents I was sitting in. I also remember that year as being the least exciting Christmas mornings because I already knew almost everything I was going to get.

In this section of his letter, James provides ample references as he points to three champions of patience: Farmers, prophets and a man named Job. Each group will help us grasp aspects of patience that, when combined, will empower us to endure in godly patience.

Farmers: Gaining Situational Insight

My family traditionally goes apple picking in the autumn. I am still flabbergasted that this became a trend and that so many people enjoy doing it. I must just not have the same genes as the rest of my family because they adore it. It may be that I just missed the point, or maybe everyone else is just weird.

While I'm picking the apples, I often look at the sides of the apple picking bags. Depending on the orchard, there may be a schedule that details the planting and harvest schedule for certain types of fruits and vegetables to help you know when to come down and pick them. Each time I see it, I'm fascinated at the variety of growing periods and harvest times. It's obvious that a lot of thought has been put into the growing of each of these items over past centuries.

James identified with the importance that farmers must place on timing and applied it to the spiritual life. By using farmers as an example, he was not just encouraging patience for patience's sake. He was highlighting the fact that God always provides a motivation for us to be patient.

In James 5:7, we see the way that farmers demonstrate patience: "Be patient, therefore, brothers, until the coming of the Lord. See how the farmer waits for the precious fruit of the earth, being patient about it, until it receives the early and the late rains." Farmers are motivated to plant and harvest in relation to the spring (early) and autumn (late) rains because that is the ideal way to grow the best harvest. If farmers decided to plant seeds willy-nilly in October when that particular plant would be best planted in April, they wouldn't receive as much (or anything) for their efforts. No matter how badly they wanted that particular plant, they couldn't rush it along by starting the growing process earlier than the growing season would allow.

We may not always see the exact reason that God is asking for patience. In the end, the motivation that should trump all others is a desire to please him. There is no greater investment strategy than placing every filament of our need onto his altar. If done with Christ's love, we can experience the instant, aromatic release of his grace and enduring peace that emanates from the destruction of our fractured desires. Even in an extreme physical, mental or financial drought, we can soak in the enduring reality that flows from God. Let us all wait for the early and the late rains and live off of the grace we've been given in the moment.

Prophets: Enduring for God's Sake

The people who were willing to repeat God's words make up the second group that James refers us to for a lesson in patience. While we don't get a bulleted list of the prophets that were being referenced, almost all of them are great examples. By not singling out a specific prophet, his statement infers that everyone who brought God's word had a measure of God-given patience that helped them endure the hardship and abuse that came with danger for prophets. Those who are given God's word to shout out must rely on patience to be spurred on to their goals.

In most cases, God's prophets were mistreated and rejected in at least one period of their ministry. After all, the words they had to say were not very palatable and were given to callous audiences. Messages of repentance and warning are not crowd-pleasing. Jesus, who, before he came to earth, had sent the prophets to his people in order to warn them and protect them, knew of the atrocities that were done against his messengers. While in the midst of a group of Israel's religious leaders near the temple during his time on earth, Jesus gave an emotional speech that contained this section about the prophets:

> Woe to you, scribes and Pharisees, hypocrites! For you build the tombs of the prophets and decorate the monuments of the righteous, saying, "If we had lived in the days of our fathers, we would not have taken part with them in shedding the blood of the prophets." Thus you witness against yourselves that you are sons of those who murdered the prophets. (Matthew 23:19-31)

Jesus went on to lament about the way that the prophets were treated in the capital of Judah: "O Jerusalem, Jerusalem, the city that kills the prophets and stones those who are sent to it!" (Matthew 23:37a).

By telling us to examine the prophets as representations of patience, James gives us a high bar to reach. He specifically calls out all of the people throughout history who heard God's voice and proclaimed it, no matter the cost to themselves or their families. They spoke in God's name and glorified him above all in displays of love and admiration that each of us should desire to echo.

The determining factor in the success of the prophet's patience was in the revelations that they received from God. In 2 Peter 1:21, Peter describes to us how the prophets were able to continue in their ministry: "For no prophecy was ever produced by the will of man, but men spoke from God as they were carried along by the Spirit.". This meant that they had partnered with the Holy Spirit in order to do the will of God. The strength came from their willingness to speak what the Holy Spirit desired for them to proclaim. Our own will cannot conjure up the strength necessary to keep us going. We must be listening to the spirit and reflecting what he has for us to share.

By consistently seeking God in their daily lives, God gave them spiritual light for them to see him more clearly. The more they saw, the less they were distracted from their goal. God turned on a beacon in the darkness of their hearts and they swam toward it with all of their hearts, minds and strength. They performed impossible feats of patience that were made reality through this God-given revelation and the strength it gave them.

Boldness and steadfastness are required for the blessing that awaits God's people. Each one of us can receive compassion and grace from God to continue on. If we are to follow the example of the prophets' patience, our main goal must be to pray for God to give us continued revelation of himself and to share that insight with others.

Job: Becoming the Grandmaster of Patience

If there were an award for Most Patient Man of All Time, Job would be the winner. Chronologically nestled in the middle of the events of Genesis, his story is one of the oldest in the Bible and also one of the most troublesome to ponder. It throws a rather large monkey wrench into the idea that being a Christian will bring always bring blessing and happiness.

At the beginning of the book named after him, Job had a decent sized family and had political and social clout. God's blessing had made him affluent. We don't know how long it took him to build up his wealth, but we do know at that he had large herds of various animals. His wealth was so immense that he was called "the greatest of all the people of the east" (Job 1:3). His success hinged on his relationship with God. He "feared God and turned away from evil" (Job 1:1b) and continually went out of his way to worship God as his first priority, providing sacrifices for his children because he knew that they had probably sinned during one of their celebrations. In other words, Job was loaded, happy and put God at the center of his life.

His patience and commitment to God was tested in a way that has caused much debate and consternation among Christians and scholars. Whether allegorical or spiritually real, the devil had a conversation with God in which the devil challenged Job's faith because, he said, "Does Job fear God for no reason? Have you not put a hedge around him and his house and all that he has, on every side? You have blessed the work of his hands, and his possessions have increased in the land. But stretch out your hand and touch all that he has, and he will curse you to your face" (Job 1:9b-11).

God allowed the devil to have power over various areas of Jobs life. Within a short period of time, a multitude of catastrophes fell upon Job. He became childless, penniless, covered in sores, and surrounded by hostile friends and a bickering wife who told him, "Do you still hold fast your integrity? Curse God and die" (Job 2:7b). If we put ourselves in the perspective of Job at the moment where he lost everything, his response to the calamity that had rushed upon him is both astonishing and overwhelming:

> Then Job arose and tore his robe and shaved his head and fell on the ground and worshiped. And he said, "Naked I came from my mother's womb, and naked shall I return. The Lord gave, and the Lord has taken away; blessed be the name of the Lord." In all this Job did not sin or charge God with wrong (Job 1:20-22)

What was the point of all this? Bob Sorge, who was a pastor and worship leader, was once asked the question, "Can you find a God of mercy in the book of Job?" He wrote back and said, "God could have left Job alone." In his inspirational short video titled "God Could Have Left Job Alone", Bob discusses the incredible suffering that he experienced after an accident permanently damaged his voice to the point where he could not sing and may only ever be able to speak for about an hour a day for the rest of his life. Not only did he experience physical suffering but also the emotional turmoil of a shattered identity. He was a pastor who couldn't preach and a worship leader who couldn't sing. For the next five years while he worked his way up to speaking for an hour a day, his prayer was three simple words: "I love you." Though he didn't understand why the accident happened or why God hadn't healed him yet, he let patience rule in his heart and set his focus on the eternal joys and satisfaction of God that far outweighed the temporary difficulties. He, like Job, would rather be in God's presence with a horde of issues and suffering than be completely comfortable and without God.

At the end of the story, God honored Job because of his patience. God even gave him back twice as much as he had before and compassionate family members finally came to embrace and comfort him. However, the point of the story was not the immense blessing that followed the trial. The biggest blessing came within the testing itself. Job forged an iron relationship with God that did not bend even when his situation became unbearable. He held onto what he knew to be true and did not waver from his conviction that a relationship with God was worth going through misery.

With all this talk of patience and sticking with it, you may have been reminded of your personal track record of patience and aren't impressed by what you see. How can you possibly live up to all of these great examples that James has given us?

There is a promise from God nestled among the many appeals to patience in this section: "You have heard of the steadfastness of Job, and you have seen the purpose of the Lord, how the Lord is compassionate and merciful" (James 5:11). Notice that when he talks about Job's steadfastness, he says, "You have heard..." because Job died thousands of years before his audience was born. However, when he mentions the purpose of the Lord, he says, "...and you have seen...", meaning that Christians have more than just historical knowledge of how God interacted with people in the past. This Christian audience was experiencing the nature of God every day and James was reminding them of the grace of God that they were already encountering.

God's promise of compassion and mercy in this excerpt from Isaiah below was fulfilled in Jesus, so all who follow God now can take hold of this promise as being activated:

> For a people shall dwell in Zion, in Jerusalem; you shall weep no more. He will surely be gracious to you at the sound of your cry. As soon as he hears it, he answers you. And though the Lord give you the bread of adversity and the water of affliction, yet your Teacher will not hide himself anymore, but your eyes shall see your Teacher. And your ears shall hear a word behind you, saying, 'This

is the way, walk in it,' when you turn to the right or when you turn to the left (Isaiah 30:19-21).

No matter how far you feel from being able to maintain patience and stick with what you promised, God is there to help and guide you with his compassionate and merciful character. He is not oblivious to the impatience and inconsistency that you have been exhibiting. Rather than holding this against you, he is running alongside you with a cool drink of compassion and mercy. You may be exhausted and are still raw from the thousands of times that you've tripped, but God is still with you as the best coach and cheerleader you could ever ask for. I don't mean this in any irreverent way. After all, it was Jesus' idea to become a servant in order to give you the chance for eternal life. He will see you through to the end if you are willing to run with him and accept the cool cups of compassion and mercy when they are offered. This is the only hope you have to sustain patience, and this hope is founded in God's eternal nature. He's not going away anytime soon and, if you extend your hand to him, he is willing to help you become the next grandmaster of patience.

Loyal Promises

In the final verse concerning patience, James 5:12 shows us how seriously we should take making promises: "But above all, my brothers, do not swear, either by heaven or by earth or by any other oath, but let your 'yes' be yes and your 'no' be no, so that you may not fall under condemnation."

When I was first organizing this book, I put this verse in its own section because I thought it wasn't really related to patience. At one point, while reading it in context, I realized that it correlates exactly with patience. What can be more demanding for our patience than following through on everything we said we would do? Sometimes our promises are easy to follow through on, and sometimes they're incredibly difficult, but the issue is exacerbated by the fact that most of us are too loose with our tongues and make promises that have no real meaning to us. This weaves back into the discussion of the tongue in chapter 3. If our hearts are not planted in a rock-solid conviction of what we should and should not be doing, we will be more easily drawn to say "yes" or "no" quickly to things that we should have considered first. I've ranked up quite a lot of points in this category, to my shame. There have been many times where I didn't follow through with what I said I would do or broke a promise that I would not do something.

James is speaking about two different topics here. First, he warns us against making rash promises. It is simple to make a promise, especially when it doesn't seem like it'll be difficult to complete, but we are tested in the act of following through. The second topic ties in with what he was speaking about in chapter 3. We learned in chapter 3 how powerful the tongue is and if we disregard that power, it is like we are absentmindedly waving a loaded gun around. King Solomon discussed the importance of promises in Ecclesiastes:

> When you vow a vow to God, do not delay paying it, for he has no pleasure in fools. Pay what you vow. It is better that you should not vow than that you should vow and not pay. Let not your mouth lead you into sin, and do not say before the messenger that it was a mistake. Why should God be angry at your voice and destroy the work of your hands? For when dreams increase and words grow many, there is vanity; but God is the one you must fear. (Ecclesiastes 5:4-7)

When Jesus came onto the scene, he provided a new perspective on our words. James' words echo a warning that Jesus gave in Matthew concerning the evil that comes from misusing words: "Let what you say be simply 'Yes' or 'No'; anything more than this comes from evil" (Matthew 5:37).

From this, we see that we should no longer rely on special words and phrases like "I swear to God", "Yes, I promise" or "I give my word" to make promises. Instead, we are to give a simple "yes" or "no" as a response. This is a difficult habit to break now that we've been inundated with the lie that we have to "swear" to do something. Jesus is not letting us off the hook here from saying "yes" or "no" to certain actions; he is saying when we say "yes" or "no", we take our word seriously and not back out when it becomes inconvenient. Our "yes" and "no" are binding contracts that have consequences if they are broken or bent.

Next time you are asked to make a commitment, no matter how small it is, take some time to think it through. When you decide upon a reply, give a simple yes or no along with a genuine explanation. Don't answer too quickly and don't be non-committal. Also, don't give reasons that aren't honest or only tell part of the truth. It may feel like mental torture at first if you're used to another way of handling requests, but if you stick with it, you will develop a good reputation and a pure conscience. "A good name is to be chosen rather than great riches, and favor is better than silver or gold" (Proverbs 22:1).

The sweet spot is a delicate balance between the two extremes of over promising and bowing out of everything. If we are to be effective Christians, we must walk along this narrow cliff edge each day, asking God to give us wisdom on how to navigate each day's terrain. Instead of being loose with our promises or being completely non-committal, let us make decisions wisely and follow through with them.

Reflection, Prayer and Action

- **Reflection**: When was the last time you had to wait for something? How well did you handle it? Have you been confronted with a difficult situation where you had to decide whether or not to stick with a promise that you made?
- **Prayer**: "God, help me to embrace patience in my life. I know that if I rely on you, you will take care of me. You are the righteous judge and I wait patiently for your timing. I look to the examples of patience that you've given me and I eagerly follow their example."
- **Action**: Take some time to familiarize yourself with one of the examples of patience that James mentioned. Pick one or two areas of their life to emulate this week.

JAMES 5:13-18
Releasing Life through Community

"Is anyone among you suffering? Then he must pray. Is anyone cheerful? He is to sing praises. Is anyone among you sick? Then he must call for the elders of the church and they are to pray over him, anointing him with oil in the name of the Lord; and the prayer offered in faith will restore the one who is sick, and the Lord will raise him up, and if he has committed sins, they will be forgiven him. Therefore, confess your sins to one another, and pray for one another so that you may be healed. The effective prayer of a righteous man can accomplish much. Elijah was a man with a nature like ours, and he prayed earnestly that it would not rain, and it did not rain on the earth for three years and six months. Then he prayed again, and the sky poured rain and the earth produced its fruit."
– James 5:13-18 NASB

"In prayer it is better to have a heart without words than words without a heart."
– John Bunyan

Responding to Circumstances

Victor Frankl, the author of Man's Search for Meaning, wrote this concerning the response that we, as humans, can have to any situation: "The one thing you can't take away from me is the way I choose to respond to what you do to me. The last of one's freedoms is to choose one's attitude in any given circumstance." These two sentences are made even more poignant when we know the story behind them. Frankl and his family, who were German Jews, were torn from their homes and split apart during WWII. Frankl was tossed, alone, into a concentration camp called Kaufering (which was affiliated with Dachau) where he was tortured, mistreated, starved and overworked. His entire family, including his wife, brother, and mother, were killed in various ways, leaving only one sister who had escaped to Australia. This man was physically and emotionally beat up and seemed to have every right to just give up. However, he was still determined that he – and everyone else – had the ability to decide his own response in every situation, no matter how hard the circumstance.

In this section of his letter, James commends a variety of actions to relate to the different situations that his readers may be experiencing. While the circumstances change, his recommendations all lead to one thing: Direct interaction with God. Whether through praying, praising, confessing sins or seeking help from fellow Christians, they are acts of worship that build our relationship with God. They are also actions that aren't the most pleasant or first to come to mind.

When I am experiencing emotional, physical or mental suffering, my tendency is not to immediately pray, even though I have been trying to train myself to make that my first thought. More often than I'd like to admit, I get into a slump and start watching a movie, distracting myself on my phone, or doing something creative or positive only for the sake of getting my mind off of whatever was bothering me. In light of the way others have handled the most intense sufferings for Jesus, my reactions could not seem more childish. One particular man named Richard Wurmbrand is a chief example of how prayer is possible and even necessary in suffering. He was a Christian during the Communist reign in Russia and spent many years in prison being tortured because he believed in Jesus. This is part of his account concerning his time in captivity:

> In solitary confinement, we could not pray as before. We were unimaginably hungry; we had been drugged until we acted like idiots. We were as weak as skeletons. The Lord's Prayer was much too long for us; we could not concentrate enough to say it. My only prayer repeated again and again was, 'Jesus, I love You.' And then, one glorious day I got the answer from Jesus: 'You love me? Now I will show you how I love you.' At once, I felt a flame in my heart, which burned like the coronal streamers

of the sun. The disciples on the way to Emmaus said that their hearts burned when Jesus spoke with them. So it was with me. I knew the love of the One who gave His life on the cross for us all (Richard Wurmbrand, *Tortured For Christ*).

Praying during suffering is certainly more work initially because we are forced to confront the negative feelings, hairy situation or sinful nature that is mixed up in the suffering. Without fail, within a minute or two of praying, part of the weight of the situation starts to lift and, even if nothing has changed, a new perspective or grace is often given. Every problem melts away under the blazing glory of eternity in joy with Jesus. No matter how broken, pressured, scared, hurt or stressed you are, there is a better future beyond the borders of your life. Keep at it and live this life in Christ, praying at every opportunity you have to receive help from God now and a continued hope for the future that cannot be destroyed.

When I'm happy and everything is going my way, my first instinct is usually not to praise God for his blessings. Instead, I revel in the emotional high for a while before I remember to thank God for his grace. After all, the joy that we feel comes from God, but we were not meant to merely experience it. In *Reflections on the Psalms*, C.S. Lewis helps us see what praise is in a new light that may change your perspective forever:

> I think we delight to praise what we enjoy because the praise not merely expresses but completes the enjoyment; it is its appointed consummation. It is not out of compliment that lovers keep on telling one another how beautiful they are; the delight is incomplete till it is expressed… If it were possible for a created soul fully… to "appreciate", that is to love and delight in, the worthiest object of all, and simultaneously at every moment to give this delight perfect expression, then that soul would be in supreme beautitude… The Scotch catechism says that man's chief end is "to glorify God and enjoy Him forever". But we shall then know that these are the same thing. Fully to enjoy is to glorify. In commanding us to glorify Him, God is inviting us to enjoy Him.

When James encourages us to sing praise, he is not merely requiring us to give praise where praise is due. He is saying, "Praise God in your cheerfulness and you will expand your capacity for joy."

Cheerfulness seems to fall to the wayside when I get sick. Being really sick means being vulnerable, and at least for me, it is the time where I would most like to be by myself. Asking for church leadership and other Christians to pray for me through text seems a lot easier and less invasive than having them come over to pray for me.

Lastly, and usually least pleasant at first, is the act of confessing our sins to a few trustworthy Christians. Even if there is no possibility that person will air our dirty laundry, the initial dread of exposing our internal darkness can be daunting. Many have decided to keep at least some of their sins hidden and would rather they fester and boil in secret than be healed in the vulnerability of the light. Don't allow yourself to become one of those people who hide their sins from everyone. If you do that, you may be blocking part of the healing process that Jesus paid so dearly to give to you.

Because we, as Christians, are the body of Christ, acting together to expose and deal with sin is not just one person helping another. When we work with other Christians in this way, we are letting Jesus come into the situation and are really working with him.

Every Moment Thirsts for Prayer

While James does spend some time encouraging diverse forms of worship, in this section he is mostly interested in prayer. This leads us to ask a question that has puzzled many new Christians, scholars and unbelievers for thousands of years. Why should we pray? If God is almighty and benevolent, why should we pray?

The first reason is the simplest and most inspiring reasons I have ever found: Because God told us many times to pray. Commands, examples, and sweet songs throughout the Old and New Testaments are riddled with reminders that God desires for us to pray. I am tempted to stop with this first point, but that would keep us from seeing the purpose behind God's instruction.

The second reason for praying is that God enjoys having us involved in his plan. God has given us much more than a simple command that must be followed blindly, so I cannot just end there. God is not like a parent who simply tells his children what to do and what not to do. There are times when he doesn't explain himself directly, and we should be content in those moments. Nevertheless, we must not give up on trying to uncover the mysteries of God and prayer.

The third reason for praying is to allow us to see in the same way that God sees. God says to us, "Call to me and I will answer you, and will tell you great and hidden things that you have not known" (Jeremiah 33:3). Like night vision goggles for the soul, prayer helps us to know what we couldn't have before. Elijah, who was a prophet in the Old Testament, was one of the great role models for this. Because of his consistent communion with God, he was available and ready to hear God's voice whenever he was called. We see once instance of the fruits of Elijah's prayers in 1 Kings 18:1: "After many days the word of the Lord came to Elijah, in the third year, saying, 'Go, show yourself to Ahab, and I will send rain upon the earth.'"

Elijah was able to hear God's calling because he was putting himself in a place of receptive prayerfulness. I see a substantial amount of evidence in the Bible – and in personal experience – that prayer brings a new layer of understanding and holy prioritization into everyday life. When we pray consistently, we will begin to see all the ways in which we can better serve God and live an authentic Christian lifestyle as laid out in James and the rest of the New Testament.

The question then becomes "How often should I pray?" If prayer is so important, what kind of time commitment should we give to it? The simple and strange answer comes from the Apostle Paul in one of his letters: "Rejoice always, pray without ceasing, give thanks in all circumstances; for this is the will of God in Christ Jesus for you" (1 Thessalonians 5:16-18).

When I first tried to grasp the command to "pray without ceasing", I quickly realized that my paradigm was not suited to understand it or make it happen. My understanding of prayer was specific times each day. I needed a God-sized paradigm to accomplish a prayer schedule that never threw in the towel. James only gives us a few examples of when to pray, but in his usual to-the-point way he covers all the bases and effectively echoes Paul's command to pray without ceasing. I don't know about you, but there are rarely times where I'm not suffering, cheerful, sick or sinning. By telling us to reach out to God in each of those circumstances, James is inferring that every moment thirsts for prayer.

Angela and I have been married for a few years now. We intentionally set aside a specific time each day to discuss how everything is going, which is very important to our relationship. That time allows us to unwind a little bit, get to know each other better, and help each other if need be. However, that is not the only time we talk each day. Whenever we're both home, we have a whole bunch of different conversations ranging from diaper duty to home maintenance decisions to sharing something we found hysterical. Having a set time to talk each day enables us to keep our relationship healthy and consistent, but it is only the starting point. The rest of our little talks throughout the day are what really makes our relationship a relationship. If we did not talk throughout the day, we would be missing out on so much that the other had to offer and wouldn't be building a healthy marriage.

In the same way, when you recast the role of prayer as a necessity for relationship with God, the fog clears away a bit and you can see how praying without ceasing is possible. Instead of viewing prayer as an obligation, ritual, or a once-a-day vitamin that you have to swallow, you get to view it as a way to share your fears, hopes, stresses, concerns and excitement with the one who loves you more than anyone else. Share the monumental and the insignificant, the highs and the rock bottom. When prayer becomes an unending conversation, you will strengthen your relationship with God. It's all about placing your dreams and worries at his feet, strengthening your spiritual vision, and asking him to intervene with his blessing, encouragement and correction.

While this lifestyle of prayer sounds romantic, it's far from effortless. It means that you don't hold back, don't ever stop, and always expand upon the conversation. I don't know about you, but I find myself at a loss just a few hours into a conversation with someone. Now that we know the mechanics of this type of prayer, how do we sustain it? Way back in James 1:5-8, we see the rock-bottom foundation of effective prayer: Faith. Specifically, we looked into the difference between the prayer of faith and double-minded, empty words. We see reflection of those verses in this section as well. In fact, we see the words "prayer of faith" explicitly listed here to remind us what kind of prayer we are meant to pray.

This should not be condemning for those who feel that they're not walking in faith every waking moment. If that were the intention here, we would all be hopeless. Rather, it is just another opportunity for us to throw up our arms in surrender and say, "Father please strengthen me! Please help me to do what I cannot do on my own!" Incidentally, this is an exercise of our faith in and of itself. When we accept our identity in Christ, it stops being a struggle to be better and becomes a constant reminder to accept the perfect character that we have been given through the redemption in Christ.

God's Rain Comes through Prayer

Elijah was given a task that seems impossible: He was instructed to pray that it wouldn't rain in Israel until God told him to pray again for rain. This was God's response to the wickedness of the current king, Ahab, and in order to show his glory and power. In both accounts in Kings and Chronicles, Ahab is noted to be an evil ruler who promoted the worship of false gods that he borrowed from the surrounding nations. For several years after God worked through Elijah's prayer to stop the rain, God took care of Elijah and those who came into contact with him.

Three years and six months into the drought, God gave Elijah the go-ahead to pray for rain to come back to Israel. While James gives us a high-level summary of Elijah's prayer, we can go to 1 Kings for the climax of the story. After an incredible "my God versus your god" faceoff between Elijah and Ahab's false prophets - which God decisively won - Elijah turned to Ahab under a clear sky and boldly declared, "Go up, eat and drink, for there is a sound of the rushing of rain" (1 Kings 18:41). Each time I read that verse, the weight of Elijah's faith pulls at my heart and Jesus' words attempt to shatter my tiny reality: "Why are you afraid, O you of little faith?" and "Truly, I say to you, whoever says to this mountain, 'Be taken up and thrown into the sea,' and does not doubt in his heart, but believes that what he says will come to pass, it will be done for him." (Matthew 8:26, Mark 11:23). At this point, there was still no cloud in the sky or any other indication that it would rain. Elijah, filled with faith, did not wait until he saw the clouds rolling in from the sea to tell the king that it was going to rain. The statement that he made to Ahab and the prayer that followed were an extension of his faith in God.

James 5:18 gives an abridged account of the event: "Then [Elijah] prayed again, and heaven gave rain, and the earth bore its fruit." In this snippet, we see the process in which God brought his blessing: First Elijah prayed, then the heavens gave rain, and then the earth bore its fruit. I found the phrasing of this sentence to be quite interesting. Why did James go through the trouble of expressing the outcome of Elijah's prayer in such a way?

Let's analyze this for a minute. In the context of 1 Kings 18, Elijah was instructed to pray specifically for rain. Rain was certainly needed in order to grow the crops that the people so desperately needed to survive. However, Elijah's prayer was not limited to asking for God to grow those crops. Instead, he was instructed to pray for rain. In one sense, this meant that Elijah was praying for food and other natural blessings that rain brings. In another more symbolic sense, this was an invitation for God's presence to come back into Israel. For quite some time, the rulers had been defiling the country by worshiping false gods and denying the existence and rights of God to be worshiped. The land needed the spiritual rain of God's presence. In the Bible, the Holy Spirit's coming is sometimes described in terms of rain. For example, the "pouring out" of the Holy Spirit at Pentecost in Acts 2:17 reflects the type of gushing, "late rain" mentioned in James 5:7 that usually occurred in Israel as a catalyst for a luscious harvest.

This is what God is saying to us through his instruction for Elijah to pray for rain: "I want you to pray for specific things and exact blessings. I want to give you practical things like food to eat, shelter, water, caring friends and a flourishing church. But above all I desire for you to ask me for my presence. I want to be invited into your lives. I want you to be healthy, but more than anything I want to have a relationship with you." His presence is the only thing that can truly satisfy us; the only thing that we are really looking for through all other blessings. All satisfaction and pleasure emanate from God, as we learned in James 1:17. When we seek God on a consistent basis, our lives become saturated with his presence. This often does not mean that we will become millionaires, successful overnight, or well liked by everyone. It does not mean that God is our own personal piggy bank or that he is willing to give us everything that we ask, even if it will hurt us. It means that we will start to see things the way that God sees them.

I pray that we always seek God's blessing in the same way that Elijah did, asking for the substance of God to rain down on us, knowing that he will provide sustenance that will help us endure.

Community

In the study of biology, we learn that the ongoing processes that are required to sustain most life are digestion, circulation, movement, excretion, respiration, reproduction, immunity, coordination, and synthesis. This is, of course, what you are reading this book to learn, right? While I was teaching Biology to a group of homeschoolers years ago, I explored each of these life processes with the class and discussed how each of them work together to make healthy, thriving organisms. For example, digestion allows for the breakdown of food into nutritious molecules while coordination helps various functions work together in efficient ways.

In the midst of James' directives concerning prayer, there is an undercurrent that revolves around community that should not be ignored. Most prominently, he encourages us to reach out to church leaders and other Christians when we are sick and to confess our sins to each other because it promotes healing.

While we have been discussing prayer as an individual activity between us and God, there is also a person-to-person element that brings communal potency to our prayers. Does it seem odd to you that part of the process of prayer involves other people? It still does to me, but it is an oddness that shows the nature of the love and glory of God. God, bringing Father, Son and Holy Spirit in one, is in a constant state of relationship with himself and we were designed to reflect that. We are meant to work together as one organism in the service of Christ and for the good of each other. In a way, each of us in the body of Christ carry out various life processes that keep the overall organism functioning properly. In context of this section of James, there are leaders who have been selected by the church and tasked with the life process of circulation. As a life process, circulation involves bringing materials to where they are needed in order to promote health. In the body of Christ, prayer performs many life functions and, in the case of church leadership, it ushers the life of God into situations that require healing.

Confessing our sins to one another is another curious but beautiful life function in every authentic Christian community. When it is performed among people we have decided to trust, it can be incredibly restorative. We get a glimpse of this in John's first epistle: "But if we walk in the light, as he is in the light, we have fellowship with one another, and the blood of Jesus his Son cleanses us from all sin" (1 John 1:7). To put this in biological terms, this cleansing process involves excretion (waste removal) that gets rid of the junk in our souls. It unclogs our arteries to allow for good circulation. I realized the usefulness of this when I heard about my dad's adventure at the acupuncturist years ago. He had been having some pain in his lower back and was trying a few things to see what would help. The acupuncturist spent a little time evaluating him and then, with little ceremony, started jabbing a needle into my dad's lower back with machinegun speed. Needless to say, my dad highlighted how painful this was in his account. The acupuncturist then took a small glass bowl, lit a piece of paper on fire inside it, and placed it face-down on the area that had just been Swiss cheesed. After a short time, the acupuncturist took the bowl off of my dad's back and brought it up to his face so he could see. To his amazement, the bottom of the bowl was coated with a black, tar-like substance. The acupuncturist - who only spoke very broken English - grunted out, "Bad blood." My dad gathered from those two words that at some point the blood had stopped circulating in that spot and his lower back became a traffic jam where blood cells would get trapped and die. The acupuncturist had used the suction from the burning paper inside the bowl to carefully extract the mass of dead cells in my dad's back through the small needle punctures he had made. It was an undoubtedly agonizing process, but the next day my dad experienced a freedom from pain that he hadn't experienced for many months. It is the same with the process of confession. When you shine a light on your sin and show it to someone else, it may be painful and strange. You may not understand it. You may want to shy away from it. Even if it seems foreign and strange to you, let the process of confession do its proper work; let it extract the bad blood from your souls and experience the newfound freedom from pain and sin in your life.

There are certainly many other ways to compare the functions of prayer with biological life processes. To sum it up: Community, relationship and prayer are essential to an effective and authentic Christianity. This is God's effective plan for releasing life to his church.

Reflection, Prayer and Action

- **Reflection**: How is your prayer life? How often do you pray with others?
- **Prayer**: "God, I know that you love your church and I want to be part of your plan to change the world through it. Help me to join in prayer with people around me and be consistently praying for them."
- **Action**: Schedule some time to pray as a family or with your church community this week.

JAMES 5:19-20
PURSUING REDEMPTION

"My brothers, if anyone among you wanders from the truth and someone brings him back, let him know that whoever brings back a sinner from his wandering will save his soul from death and will cover a multitude of sins."
– James 5:19-20

"Hatred stirs up strife, but love covers all offenses."
– Proverbs 10:12

"Darkness cannot drive out darkness: only light can do that. Hate cannot drive out hate: only love can do that."
– Martin Luther King Jr.

Signing Off

Without so much as a goodbye, James drops these last words and walks away. Almost all of the other New Testament letters end with a request to say hello to certain people in the area, acknowledgement of God's greatness, and a benediction (blessing) for those who read the letter. Knowing James as well as we do now, this is a fitting end to his open letter to Christians.

If this letter were a song and James its conductor, it would be a flurry of big, bold notes from the very beginning with violins rapidly dancing back and forth. These two verses at the end would be the moment where every instrument blasts out the resolving note simultaneously and then immediately drop into silence. Or, if you prefer dubstep to classical music, James gets to the drop after just a few seconds and doesn't stop the persistent wall of sound and drastic highs and lows until he hits the last programmed button.

For a while, I didn't see how these last two verses were connected to the rest of the letter. It was as if James had an "Oh, I should mention this as well…" moment and hastily added a postscript. However, as we shall see, James was leading us to this moment from the first words of the letter. This is not the dry ending to a pithy sermon about being "good". These last two verses are the culmination of an adventure through the heart of Jesus and into the greatest celebration festival we will ever experience.

James ends his letter in redemption, which is fitting considering how much it is needed. As a skilled wordsmith, he weaved Jesus' honeyed words into our every-day lives in a wonderful poem that crescendos in redemption. Eternal communion with God is indeed a sweet masterpiece! Thank you, James, for bringing a reminder of that glorious light to our hearts!

Who Salvation Saves

There has been some confusion that has arisen from the last verse in this letter. In it, James says, "...let him know that whoever brings back a sinner from his wandering will save his soul from death and will cover a multitude of sins" (James 5:20). Essentially, it is saying that Christians should be aware that when they bring someone back to Christ, that person's sins are completely forgiven and they are saved from eternity in hell. Sadly, some have interpreted this verse like this: "If I bring someone back to Jesus, I will secure my own salvation." While this sounds like the right thing to do to gain favor with God and justly earn our salvation, the thought behind it is rooted in a misunderstanding of the gospel. It is a lie. As I've stated several times in this book, our salvation is not earned through our actions but instead is founded in personal belief in Christ. Naturally, that belief in Christ grows in us the motivation and power to bring people back to Christ, but the action itself does not ensure our salvation; it merely proves to us that we are already saved.

Another more difficult topic arises from those two simple verses: If a Christian wanders, does that cancel out their salvation? If a confessing believer stops following in the path of Christ, must he be brought to Christ in order to receive salvation? The simple answer to this question is "No", but we will need to go through the details to discover why.

Firstly, note that I said "confessing believer", not "believer". Throughout his letter, James uses the word "brothers" to appeal to those who believe themselves to be Christians. James desires that all who identify themselves as Christians are in fact saved, but this is not the case. There will be those who falsely claim, or even wholeheartedly believe, that they've placed Jesus as the lord of their lives and yet do not have salvation. Jesus made this clear during his Sermon on the Mount: "Not everyone who says to me, 'Lord, Lord,' will enter the kingdom of heaven, but the one who does the will of my Father who is in heaven" (Matthew 7:21).

This is an important distinction primarily in the light of the "once saved, always saved" doctrine, which I believe. This doctrine states that once a person receives salvation, nothing and no one can tear that salvation from them, not even their own actions. So, conversely, how can we claim that someone has not received salvation even though they have confessed Jesus as their savior? If they identify themselves as "brothers", how can they not have salvation? Initially, this seems to fly in the face of that doctrine. However, once we refer to our discussion on faith earlier, the vista becomes clearer. If we tie this back to the section in chapter 2 that discusses faith and works, we see that dead faith and hollow belief exist: "For as the body apart from the spirit is dead, so also faith apart from works is dead" (James 2:26). There are several examples of this in scripture. We don't know how the people eventually fared, but these people evidently ran away from Christ at one point to chase their own happiness outside of God:

> For Demas, in love with this present world, has deserted me and gone to Thessalonica (2 Timothy 4:10).

> They went out from us, but they were not of us; for if they had been of us, they would have continued with us. But they went out, that it might become plain that they all are not of us (1 John 2:19).

Even Jesus was rejected by many of his followers when he taught them some truth that they couldn't stomach:

> After this many of his disciples turned back and no longer walked with [Jesus] (John 6:66).

While it is frightening to me that someone who got so close to the truth ended up rejecting it and running away from it, it is disturbing to think that there are people who are "wolves in sheep's clothing" who have found Christianity to be useful to their own ends. They play the game, check the boxes, get praised by those around them, and yet are completely devoid of God's life. By far the most terrifying thought to me is that there are those out there who are convinced of their own salvation and yet have not obtained it. Whether because of their own laziness and lack of desire to read the truths in the Bible or because of the lies that they were told, they are walking corpses and don't know it.

What does this all mean for us? Should these dire circumstances make us question our own salvation? Since only God knows who is truly saved, this seems like a lost cause. However, as Christians who have genuinely received saving faith, we have no reason to doubt. We will always have questions and concerns, and will ideally spend a significant amount of time trying to put together the puzzle of our beliefs, theology and doctrines in a way that honors God. There is no shame in experiencing doubt and terror at the possibility of our beliefs being misguided, but it is what we do with those feelings that makes the difference. There may even be times when we completely lose our way and try to live as a refugee from the truth. It is God's plan for sanctification that keeps on bringing those whom God has chosen back to him. Our responsibility is to fall at Jesus' feet with our concerns and ask him to assure us again of our salvation.

In the letter of 1 John, the author uses his last chapter to help us to be sure in our faith: "Everyone who believes that Jesus is the Christ has been born of God, and everyone who loves the Father loves whoever has been born of him" (1 John 5:1). His desire was to help us avoid constant fear that we did not receive salvation: "I have written these things to you who believe in the name of the Son of God so that you may know that you have eternal life" (1 John 5:13). In the ultimate assurance of our salvation, Jesus says, "I give them eternal life, and they will never perish, and no one will snatch them out of my hand" (John 10:28).

Now that we've laid down a foundation, let's examine what James is talking about here: "My brothers, if anyone among you wanders from the truth and someone brings him back, let him know that whoever brings back a sinner from his wandering will save his soul from death and will cover a multitude of sins" (James 5:19-20).

I would contend that those who claim to have been converted and yet end up eternally rejecting Jesus at some point have not yet received salvation. The saving faith that Christians receive through Christ results in growth, no matter how quickly or slowly it comes. If saving faith never actually came, that person may have just been going on their own until he or she ran out of juice and, in frustration, gave up on it altogether. Or that person may have used a bastardized form of Christianity for his own gain (true Christianity never focuses on personal gain outside of Christ). Lastly, he may still walk in dark denial about his lack of salvation, which will cause him to blindly stray away from the truth. The hope here is that people have not received salvation and yet have not eternally rejected God. They are simply those who came into a situation where they mentally ascended to the gospel and, because they didn't receive saving faith, gave up on it, distorted it, or blindfolded themselves.

Most of what I just said becomes completely irrelevant to our daily lives because we cannot, without God's guidance, differentiate between the different conditions of people who appear to have walked away from Christ. Because we don't know whether or not the person is actually saved (only God can know that), we ought to treat everyone who leaves the path of sanctification as if they never genuinely received Christ. We have no way of knowing, beyond revelation from the Holy Spirit, if someone is either saved but wandering, not saved and wandering, or eternally rejecting God. From a practical standpoint, our job becomes incredibly simple: We must interact with everyone who is not currently living an authentic Christian life as someone who has not actually received salvation. The only fitting way to interact with James' encouragement is to reach out to those who appear to be without the life of God.

This is not to say that we should to look down on them or treat them as less than us. On the contrary, we ought to have the ultimate compassion for them because they may have not yet been touched by life itself. After all, none of us can make salvation happen. If you look carefully at James' words, he says, "My brothers, if anyone among you wanders from the truth and someone brings him back..." Note that there is no mention of our bringing them to salvation. We are meant to bring them to the truth.

So What's the Plan?

Now that we've confirmed that we ought to bring back "a sinner from his wandering", let's explore how to do it. James doesn't explain a method in these two verses, but he did unroll the plan for redemption back in chapter 4:1-10, so this is an excellent place to start. Once we have adopted the plan ourselves we can turn around and help others apply it to their lives. The plan is to graciously and lovingly help them confront their own sin, humble themselves before God, resist the devil and the evil in their hearts, and sprint like mad to God.

Although the plan is clear, there is no magic formula that will help us deduce who will come to Christ and at what time. There are probably people who come to mind when I ask you who you know who is close to believing in Christ. It very well may be that they are close, but we are not authorized or aware enough of God's plan to judge. The religious leaders of Jesus' day seemed to be closer to God according to what they knew, but Jesus dispelled that theory: "Truly, I say to you, the tax collectors and the prostitutes go into the kingdom of God before you" (Matthew 21:31b). Rather than focusing our efforts only on people who appear to be more put together, we ought to ask God for wisdom and guidance about whom to help direct toward the truth, regardless of how open they may seem. If God guides us, we ought to spend time getting to know those around us who seem farthest from God. The surprising truth is that those who are roughest around the edges are often more likely to call upon God because they can see their own brokenness. That is why God said, "But when he heard it, he said, 'Those who are well have no need of a physician, but those who are sick. Go and learn what this means, "I desire mercy, and not sacrifice." For I came not to call the righteous, but sinners.'" (Matthew 9:12-13). Only those who discover how sick they are spiritually are going to reach out to God for healing, and it is the most broken who will likely notice this.

This task is central to our faith. In his last commandment to his disciples while in bodily form on earth, Jesus said, "Go therefore and make disciples of all nations, baptizing them in the name of the Father and of the Son and of the Holy Spirit..." (Matthew 28:19). In his commentary on James, John Calvin discusses the significance of the salvation of a wandering soul:

> Nothing is better or more desirable than to deliver a soul from eternal death; and this is what he does who restores an erring brother to the right way: therefore a work so excellent ought by no means to be neglected. To give food to the hungry, and drink to the thirsty, we see how much Christ values such acts; but the salvation of the soul is esteemed by him much more precious than the life of the body. We must therefore take heed lest souls perish through our sloth, whose salvation God puts in a manner in our hands. Not that we can bestow salvation on them; but that God by our ministry delivers and saves those who seem otherwise to be nigh destruction.

Though our task has incredible weight to it, we are not the ones who ultimately bring about salvation, so our strategy centers on patience and perseverance, always trusting that God will come through. It is not the monumental leaps that we are to be concerned about. Most likely, it is the tiny, incremental, and mostly invisible shifts in a person's soul that are the truest indicator for their eventual salvation. As C.S. Lewis put it, "Remember, we Christians think man lives forever. Therefore, what really matters is those little marks or twists on the central, inside part of the soul which are going to turn it, in the long run, into a heavenly or a hellish creature" (*Mere Christianity*). Since God is the only one who can see most of the changes in a soul, it is up to us to continue our work with steadfastness in the face of even the most outwardly hard-hearted individual or group. In my experience, drifting Christians who have incredible passion and intense opinions are probably not far from finding God, so do not discount someone who is vocally against God or is passionate about something other than God. That passion can be redirected toward a zealous Christian lifestyle that may blow you away. Complete absence of enthusiasm is a far worse enemy to conversion than misguided passion, but both can be roused to life through the prayer and consistency of a Christian.

Our part to play in the salvation process of others is stated simply and effectively in *Becoming a Contagious Christian* by Bill Hybels and Mark Mittelberg. We must have high potency toward, close proximity with, and clear communication to others in order to make maximum impact in their souls. Let's examine each of these shortly.

First, a highly potent life comes from being intentionally close to God and following all of the guidance given in James' letter as well as the rest of the New Testament. When we treat the gospel as truth in our lives, our everyday actions become persuasive messages to everyone that Jesus is alive. The strongest salt and the brightest lighthouse are destined to lead people to find God and worship him (Matthew 5:13-16).

The second element is consistent interaction with and prayer for others. When we spend time with people, pray for them, and interact with them through God's love, we simultaneously give them a glimpse of God and give ourselves a deeper desire to help them. Friendship usually comes before someone is willing to be open and vulnerable enough to listen.

Clear communication finishes up the formula for maximum impact. By reading, living and expressing truth, we become a direct line from God to those who we interact with. The difficulty is in tailoring your message to different situations without watering it down. Thankfully, even if you only get to say a few words or perform a small act that's in line with the gospel, God can take it and amplify it until it's the only thing that person sees or hears. Never underestimate your words and actions; always seek the integrity to act and speak from your identity in Christ.

When we apply this formula to our lives, we will begin to see life springing up in all kinds of places that we haven't before. Just keep pressing into it. Find ways to share the gospel that may possibly be used by God to bring them back to the truth and obtain salvation once and for all. This is the defining moment in James' letter where all that we have discussed comes into focus. We see that this is not just for us. We have the responsibility and the great joy of guiding others into the very same freedom that we've looked at, marveled in, and experienced. Let's go out and live an authentic Christian lifestyle and help others find it!

Reflection, Prayer and Action

- **Reflection**: How often do you reach out to those far from God? When you do, do you interact with love at the center of your motivation?
- **Prayer**: "God, make me the kind of person who earnestly seeks to reconcile people to you. I want to be so excited about you that I automatically share you with others. Let my words and deeds be effective ways to share your glory with others."
- **Action**: Begin praying on a regular basis for at least one person who has stopped living as a Christian.

About the Author

Everett and his wife, Angela, live in Connecticut with their daughter, Mia. When not writing a book, he finds enjoyment in spending time with family and friends, discipling, blogging, teaching and praying.

Website/Blog: www.everetth.com

Email: info@everetth.com

Twitter: www.twitter.com/everetthill

Instagram: www.instagram.com/everetthill/

Appendix A – Additional Resources to Study James

Commentaries on the Letter of James

James (MacArthur Bible Studies) by John MacArthur

Commentary on James by John Calvin

Commentary on James (Spurgeon Commentary Series) by Charles Spurgeon

Life Lessons: Book of James: Practical Wisdom (Life Lessons)

Appendix B – Resources for an Authentic Christian Life

"But the one who looks into the perfect law, the law of liberty, and perseveres, being no hearer who forgets but a doer who acts, he will be blessed in his doing."
- James 1:25

Dietrich Bonhoeffer

The Cost of Discipleship

John Bunyan

The Pilgrim's Progress

Francis Chan

Crazy Love: Overwhelmed by a Relentless God

Henry Cloud

Changes That Heal: The Four Shifts That Make Everything Better...And That Everyone Can Do

Germaine Copeland

Prayers That Avail Much

Bill Hybels and Mark Mittleberg

Becoming a Contagious Christian

C. S. Lewis

Mere Christianity

The Problem of Pain

The Screwtape Letters

The Weight of Glory

Erwin W. Lutzer

Getting to No: How to Break a Stubborn Habit

John MacArthur

The MacArthur Study Bible

John Piper

www.DesiringGod.org

Desiring God: Meditations of a Christian Hedonist

When I Don't Desire God: How to Fight for Joy

Charles Spurgeon

Morning and Evening: Daily Reading

A. W. Tozer

The Pursuit of God

Made in the USA
San Bernardino, CA
08 January 2017